W9-CER-082

THE HARLEM RENAISSANCE

AFRICAN-AMERICAN ACHIEVERS

THE HARLEM RENAISSANCE

Veronica Chambers

CHELSEA HOUSE PUBLISHERS
Philadelphia

To Michael Trotman, with gratitude and love

Chelsea House Publishers
Editor-in-Chief Stephen Reginald
Production Manager Pamela Loos
Picture Editor Judy Hasday
Art Director Sara Davis
Managing Editor Jim Gallagher
Senior Production Editor Lisa Chippendale

Staff for THE HARLEM RENAISSANCE
Senior Editor Therese De Angelis
Associate Editor Kristine Brennan
Designer Keith Trego
Picture Researcher Patricia Burns
Cover Design Keith Trego

3 5 7 9 8 6 4 2

Library of Congress Cataloging-in-Publication Data

Chambers, Veronica.
The Harlem Renaissance / Veronica Chambers.
128 pp.   cm. — (African-American achievers)
Includes bibliographical references and index.
Summary: Recounts the vibrant personalities and remarkable cultural movements that flourished in America's leading black community during the 1920s and 1930s.

ISBN 0-7910-2597-7 (hardcover)
    0-7910-2598-5 (pbk.)

1. Afro-American arts—New York (State)—New York—
Juvenile literature. 2. Arts, Modern—20th century—New
York (State)—New York—Juvenile literature. 3. Harlem
Renaissance—Juvenile literature. [1. Afro-American arts.
2. Arts, Modern—20th century. 3. Harlem Renaissance.] I.
Title. II. Series.
NX512.3.A35C48   1997
700'.89'9607307471—dc21
                                    97-20585
                                       CIP
                                        AC

Frontis: *A 1911 aerial view of
Harlem, looking east from Morn-
ingside Avenue and 145th Street.*

On the cover: Barbecue (1934)
*by Archibald Motley; Howard
University Gallery of Art*

CONTENTS

1
Stompin' at the Savoy 9

2
A Paradise of My Own People 25

3
The Talented Tenth 37

4
Home to Harlem 49

5
Renaissance Women 61

Picture Essay
Treasures of Harlem 65

6
Patrons of the Renaissance 83

7
Free Within Ourselves 99

8
The Last Leaf on the Tree 109

Further Reading   122

Index   124

AFRICAN-AMERICAN ACHIEVERS

THE BLACK COWBOYS

THE BLACK MUSLIMS

BOYZ II MEN

THE BUFFALO SOLDIERS

THE HARLEM GLOBETROTTERS

THE HARLEM RENAISSANCE

THE NEGRO LEAGUES

THE TEMPTATIONS

THE HARLEM RENAISSANCE

1

Stompin' at the Savoy

"A renaissance of American Negro literature is due; the material about us in the strange, heart-rending race tangle is rich beyond dream and only we can tell the tale and sing the song from the heart."

—W. E. B. Du Bois, 1920

THE AIR IN MANHATTAN'S Fifth Avenue Restaurant crackled with excitement. More than 300 well-dressed women and men exchanged gossip, laughed, and nervously sipped cocktails. All awaited an important announcement. On this spring evening, May 1, 1925, the editors of the National Urban League's prestigious magazine, *Opportunity: A Journal of Negro Life*, were holding an awards dinner to reveal the winners of the publication's first annual literary contest.

Over the previous months, Charles S. Johnson, the magazine's editor-in-chief, had been announcing the members of the Urban League's distinguished panel of judges. Among the decision makers

The Cotton Club Orchestra, 1925. Jazz music, invented by black musicians in New Orleans, Louisiana, hit Harlem and the rest of the country with such force that the 1920s became known as the Jazz Age.

were such respected literary figures as drama critic Alexander Woollcott and playwright Eugene O'Neill, who would win the Nobel Prize for literature 11 years later. James Weldon Johnson, executive secretary of the National Association for the Advancement of Colored People (NAACP), and Jessie Fauset, a noted author and literary editor of the NAACP's magazine, *The Crisis*, had also been called upon to judge. These four and 20 others had reviewed more than 730 entries in five categories: drama, poetry, short stories, essays, and personal experience. Mrs. Henry Goddard Leach, the wife of *Forum* magazine's editor, had donated an impressive $470 in prize money—a tantalizing sum for the time and a real boon for the financially challenged artists' community.

"No race can ever become great that has not produced a literature," James Weldon Johnson declared that evening. As the prizewinners were announced, it was clear that black America was on the verge of such greatness. Black and white guests were introduced to the young men and women who would shape not only black literature but all of American literature through the first half of the 20th century. The *Opportunity* awards dinner, the noted scholar Arnold Rampersand would say later, was "the greatest gathering of black and white literati ever assembled in one room."

Two of the award recipients had already achieved a measure of fame. Countee Cullen's poem "Shroud of Color" had appeared in H. L. Mencken's *American Mercury* magazine, and Langston Hughes, who had become known as the "busboy poet" of Washington, D.C.—while working at the Wardman Park Hotel, he had left some of his poems on the dining table of the poet Vachel Lindsay—took first prize for his poem "The Weary Blues."

Future literary stars were also winners that night. E. Franklin Frazier, who would become an esteemed

sociologist and scholar of African-American studies, received a first prize for his essay on social equality, and Howard University undergraduate Zora Neale Hurston, who would become one of the most distinctive voices in American literature, took two second prizes for her play *Color Struck* and her short story "Spunk."

The evening sparkled with possibility. Among the people with whom Langston Hughes became acquainted that night was Carl Van Vechten, one of the few whites in New York to investigate the Harlem that existed outside the whites-only jazz clubs. An influential critic, Van Vechten had begun to champion a number of black artists, including the actor and singer Paul Robeson, and he and his wife frequently invited black and white artists, writers, publishers, and agents to parties in their home, attempting to bring the two races together in New York. Van Vechten was so taken with Hughes and his work that, 17 days after the awards dinner, he had convinced Alfred Knopf, his own publisher, to offer Hughes a contract for a book of collected poems.

Not everyone believed that the critics' high praises of these young black writers were sincere, however. Some, like novelist Arna Bontemps, thought that the enthusiasm over the "New Negroes" was hypocritical: "Both white and Negro critics paid more attention to the fact that a writer was Negro than to the literary merit of his work," he later maintained. Others, like Eugene O'Neill, admonished the rising stars, warning them against pretension: "Be yourselves! Don't reach out for our stuff which *we* call good!"

Nevertheless, *Opportunity* magazine had clearly lived up to its name, providing a generation of blacks with a grand introduction to the literary world. It was not "a spasm of emotion," Charles Johnson remarked. "It was intended as the beginning of something and so it was." Novelist Edna Worthley Underwood, one of the contest judges, would write Charles Johnson that she saw the beginning of a new literary era in America, where the most esteemed authors would be of the "new race differently endowed."

Whatever their motivations may have been, the critics' fanfare was justified. The awards dinner was one of the key events of the Harlem Renaissance, a movement that began early in the 1920s as an asser-

A'Lelia Walker in 1925, wearing one of her many flamboyant outfits. Known for her dashing style, Walker became a prominent leader of the Harlem Renaissance.

tion of an African-American artistic and cultural identity. In a period when the United States was entrenched in segregation and racial violence, black writers, singers, poets, painters, and musicians settled in Harlem, in the northern part of New York City's Manhattan borough, and created one of the greatest cultural outpourings in American history. The neighborhood's social scene, its glamorous nightlife, and, above all, its art and literature became the nucleus of a nationwide black revolution that would transform American culture.

The 1920s were a prosperous time, and black

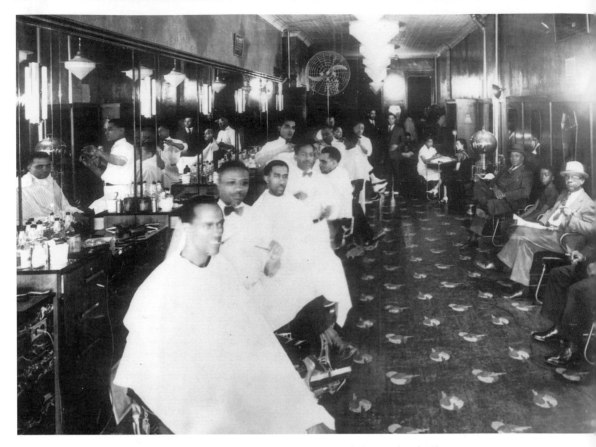

A thriving black-owned barber shop in Harlem, circa 1929. In the 1920s, Harlem became a refuge for African Americans seeking economic independence and freedom from racism.

Americans benefited from the booming economy in ways that were previously unimaginable in a segregated society. Madam C. J. Walker, the daughter of former slaves, rose from an impoverished childhood to become America's first black female millionaire by inventing a new hair-care preparation for black women. After her death in 1919, her only daughter, A'Lelia Walker, became something of a local legend, famous for her flamboyant style and lavish, celebrity-studded gatherings.

At her retreat on the Hudson River, Walker dazzled the artistic and intellectual elite of Harlem, both black and white. Believing that black artists and writers needed a comfortable forum in which to discuss their work and views, she converted her mansion on West 136th Street into a club in 1927.

The Dark Tower, as it was dubbed, took its name from poet Countee Cullen's *Opportunity* column of the same name, and a framed copy of "The Weary Blues" hung on the wall of its central room.

A striking woman who stood six feet tall and dressed in the finest silks and furs, A'Lelia Walker enjoyed having a good time—and making a statement. At one famous party, "the joy-goddess of Harlem 1920s" (as Langston Hughes called her) planned the menu as a deliberate reverse of black and white stereotypical fare. White guests were served pig's feet, chitterlings, and bathtub gin, usually thought of as poor black southerners' food, while black guests, who were seated in a more ornate dining room, feasted on caviar, pheasant, and champagne, considered the typical foods of wealthy whites.

Despite the glamorous image of the Harlem Renaissance, however, the typical Harlem resident never received an invitation to Walker's home. Many Harlemites were black southerners and African-Caribbean people who had come to New York to escape poverty. Even to poorer residents, though, Harlem in the 1920s was like a promised land. Many would write home singing the community's praises, or they would return to their former homes wearing stylish clothes and telling stories of the good life in Harlem, where black people owned their own businesses and black policemen patrolled the streets. In Harlem, free from the constant scrutiny and racism of white America, black people could be themselves.

The bravado and enthusiasm with which Walker welcomed the "New Negro Movement" was shared by nearly all Harlemites. Those who were not privileged to receive invitations to the homes of distinguished Harlemites like Walker, James Weldon Johnson, Charles Johnson, Walter White, and Reverend Frederick Cullen (Countee Cullen's adoptive father) sought cultural information at the Harlem branch of the New York Public Library and the YMCA (both on 135th Street near Lenox Avenue). In these places one could choose nearly every evening from scores of lectures, readings, debates, concerts, and dramas. The Harlem Symphony and the Harlem String Quartet performed regularly, with appearances by the renowned bandleader and arranger Fletcher Henderson, violinist Hall Johnson, pianist and composer James P. Johnson (Fats Waller's mentor), and composer and conductor William Grant Still.

Surrounding the writers of the Harlem Renaissance was a powerful resurgence of black theater. *Shuffle Along*, a musical comedy written by Eubie Blake and Noble Sissle, opened to great acclaim on Broadway in 1921. Its success led to Broadway productions of a number of other black-themed shows (often written by blacks but produced and directed by whites), including *Plantation Review*, *Chocolate Kiddies* (with music by bandleader Duke Ellington), *Dover Street to Dixie, From Dixie to Broadway*, and *Blackbirds*.

Written primarily for white audiences, many of these productions have been criticized for their stereotyped characters and minstrel-like musical numbers. Nonetheless, the shows established a number of black singers and dancers (most famously Florence Mills) as bona fide stars. Serious nonmusical theater also thrived. A number of smaller groups performed in Harlem, providing national fame for such actors as Charles Gilpin and Paul Robeson, who appeared in Eugene O'Neill's *The Emperor Jones*.

Musicals formed only part of the increasingly important black music scene. One of the era's most celebrated musical forms was jazz, the New Orleans-born sound so widely heard that novelist F. Scott Fitzgerald dubbed the 1920s "The Jazz Age." Jazz

A black dance troupe performs at Connie's Inn. Like most Harlem nightclubs during the 1920s, Connie's Inn followed Jim Crow laws that prohibited African Americans as guests.

began developing in the 1890s and early 1900s, when New Orleans was notable for its diverse ethnic mix and musical character. Around that time, local black musicians began to give popular music a new twist. Still using horns and percussion instruments, they began to "swing" the tunes—to use different times for different instruments in the band, creating a complex interplay of rhythms. The new music, known as jazz or Dixieland, was loud, brassy, and popular.

The jazz craze reached Harlem soon after that, and the explosion of new nightclubs and cabarets charged the neighborhood with musical energy. Arthur "Happy" Rhone's Black and White Club at 143rd and Lenox was the first "upstairs" club in Harlem and the first to hire waitresses and offer floor shows. Nearby, the exclusive Cotton Club boasted the orchestra of Edward Kennedy "Duke" Ellington, a suave and handsome bandleader from Washington, D.C., who had taught himself how to play the piano and composed his own band music.

Two blocks from Happy Rhone's, Fletcher Hen-

Bessie Smith, "the Empress of the Blues," captivated listeners in America and abroad with her uniquely expressive voice and her intensely dramatic singing style.

derson and his Rainbow Orchestra performed live radio broadcasts from the wildly popular Savoy Ballroom. Housed in a luxurious $200,000 block-long building stretching from 140th to 141st Street, the Savoy opened on March 12, 1926, to wild acclaim. So influential was the club in spreading the bold new musical style across the country that it was memorialized in the smash hit "Stompin' at the Savoy." David Levering Lewis relates in his book *When Harlem Was in Vogue* that "Fletcher Henderson was New York jazz in the flesh, and New York jazz—however derivative, polished, commercialized—was soon to be the dominant school as far as the record-buying, radio-listening public was concerned."

At Connie's Inn near the Lafayette Theater on Seventh Avenue, an energetic young trumpeter from New Orleans named Louis "Satchmo" Armstrong held court, playing songs such as the now classic "Ain't Misbehavin'." Born around 1900—the same time that jazz was born—Armstrong learned to play the cornet as a teenager in a reform school run by black social workers. After being discharged, he began playing at night in "honky-tonks" and later in the better jazz bands of New Orleans. His extraordinary skill attracted the attention of the city's prominent musicians: trombonist and bandleader Edward "Kid" Ory, pianist Jelly Roll Morton, and most important, cornetist and bandleader Joe "King" Oliver. In 1922, Oliver would invite Armstrong to join his Creole Jazz Band in Chicago. Two years later, Armstrong headed for New York to play with the Fletcher Henderson Orchestra. Although Armstrong remained in New York only a year, his affiliation with Henderson's orchestra helped to launch his legendary career.

The blues, or what recently transplanted black southerners referred to as "urban spirituals," also became hugely popular in Harlem during the 1920s. Originally a black folk music that used a special musical scale with certain "bent" or flat-tened notes, the slow, sensuous sound—often accompanied by suggestive lyrics—provided plenty of entertainment for the community's sophisticated nightclub audiences.

In 1923, Henderson and his orchestra teamed up with a young blues singer named Bessie Smith to record an album for Columbia Records. In songs like "Oh Daddy" and Porter Grainger's "'Tain't Nobody's Business If I Do," Smith's uniquely gritty style struck a chord with American music lovers. "That wasn't a voice she had, it was a flame-thrower licking out across the room," memoirist Mezz Mezzrow wrote of the first time he heard Bessie Smith sing. The album sold more than 700,000 copies in the six months after its release, earning Bessie Smith the title "The Empress of the Blues."

Smith recorded other hits, including "The Washerwoman's Blues," "The Workhouse Blues," and "The Empty Bed Blues," and she launched her stage and film career in 1927 with her appearance in the revue *Africana*. By that time, she had become the highest-paid black artist in the world. Although the godfathers and godmothers of the Harlem Renaissance did not approve of her earthy manner and voice, Smith was like Langston Hughes and Zora Neale Hurston in the way that she drew on African-American storytelling traditions in her songs. She avoided performing commercial show music, preferring instead to express musically the feelings and struggles of a black woman trying to make it through the day. "Smith's blues verses were poetry set to music," wrote William Barlow. "They were like all great art in that they expressed human emotions that were universal."

And in a Harlem basement club called Edmund's Cellar, Ethel Waters, a tall, brown-skinned girl known as "Sweet Mama Stringbean," made her debut. The joint was a dive—Waters

Ethel Waters (center left) with the Cotton Club chorus and Duke Ellington's Orchestra in their spring 1933 show, "Stormy Weather." A premier Harlem nightspot, the Cotton Club was eventually forced to repeal its Jim Crow policy because of Ellington's wildly popular orchestra.

would later refer to it as "the last step on the way down"—but her stint there led to her first recordings on Black Swan Records in 1921, creating hits such as "Down Home Blues."

For musician and composer Fats Waller, Harlem had always been home. His parents were active members of Harlem's Abyssinian Baptist Church. One of the era's most gifted pianists, Waller achieved success not only as a musician but also as a composer. American blues standards like "Ain't Misbehavin'," "Black and Blue," and "I've Got a Feeling That I'm Falling" are among Waller's many well-known compositions.

Despite the explosion of African-American creativity, Harlem in the 1920s was not utopia. At most of the clubs on Harlem's Jungle Alley (133rd Street)—Connie's Inn, The Nest Club, and the prestigious Cotton Club—Jim Crow laws prohibited blacks as guests. With occasional exceptions for very light-skinned African Americans who might "pass" as white, the only blacks in such clubs were hired performers.

Perhaps the flashiest and best-known Harlem nightspot was the Cotton Club, which opened in the fall of 1923. Each evening, approximately 700 white guests gathered to watch extravagant musical shows, complete with black chorus girls carrying fans and wearing glittery, feathered costumes. It was to these dancers that Cab Calloway, a frequent performer at the Cotton Club, sang such odes as "Tall, Tan, and Terrific" and "Cotton Colored Gal of Mine." Tall, muscular bouncers stood at the door to keep away Harlem residents who might try to get into the club. An often-told story describes the night that W. C. Handy, a composer from Memphis who had become known as the "Father of the Blues," was turned away from the Cotton Club while his own music was playing inside.

In an era of racial violence and prejudice, the whites-only rule was deemed essential for the success of top-dollar clubs such as the Cotton Club. Jimmy Durante, a well-known comedian, expressed the familiar prejudice of the time when he defended the exclusion of black patrons, claiming that "nobody wants razors, blackjacks or fists flying—and the chances of war are less if there's no mixing."

Although Ellington's vast popularity would eventually lead the Cotton Club to repeal its whites-only policy, the rule reflected a certain truth about Harlem's famed nightlife; namely, that whites often viewed the area as a place to escape the constraints of public opinion and "respectability" that might govern their behavior in a predominantly white area. One explanation for this view is that the clubs and cabarets of Harlem almost always served alcohol, which was illegal after 1919 when the

United States ratified the 18th, or Prohibition, Amendment to the Constitution.

The image of Harlem as a place without rules was promoted by club owners and managers, who booked exotic and ribald dancers, comedians, and singers. Among them were the notorious Gladys Bently, a female singer who impersonated a man, and Earl "Snakehips" Tucker, who gyrated his hips so fast when he danced that the whirling tassel on his belt would become a blur.

Meanwhile, Harlem's working-class residents, who were unwelcome in the clubs on Jungle Alley, found other ways of entertaining themselves—and of making ends meet as well. Rents were high in Harlem; most apartments cost $12 to $30 more per month than similar housing in other parts of Manhattan. Simply paying the rent could cost a typical working-class family 40 percent of its income. To raise money, many families took in boarders—or whooped it up at "rent parties," informal gatherings held in private homes for which admission—anywhere from a dime to 50 cents—was charged. If the party was successful, the rent could be paid for another month.

On weekends several rent parties on the same block often competed for customers, and a host's reputation for providing good liquor, good food, or good music could make or break the party. Entertainment was often amateur and arranged at a moment's notice, and aspiring jazz bands and singers got their chance for momentary recognition.

Rent parties did more than provide a good time and raise money. They helped Harlemites to develop a sense of camaraderie and fellowship in what could otherwise be an impersonal urban area. After all, the person who paid admission to a rent party might be asking others to pay for entry at her home the following week. Through these lively gatherings, people made connections, began romances, and fostered community well-being. As writer Wallace Thurman pointed out, the rent party was "as essential to 'low' Harlem as the cultural receptions and soirees . . . [were] to 'high' Harlem."

As Thurman's comment implied, black Harlem was never classless; status divided Harlemites as surely as it did downtowners. However, even those who were struggling to survive saw Harlem as a place of opportunity. A Harlemite, it was said, might be poor, but at least he was poor in Harlem. This optimism, combined with the vibrant nightlife and politics, captured the imagination of writers and intellectuals around the world.

How did Harlem become the center of a black cultural revolution? The story of the Harlem Renaissance is actually many stories: of politics and power, race and gender, and especially art, music, and literature. For perhaps the first time in American history, African Americans were able to see themselves as inheritors of an ancient culture that was richer and more varied than many could have imagined. "I am not tragically colored," Zora Neale Hurston wrote in "How It Feels to Be Colored Me." "There is no great sorrow dammed up in my soul or lurking behind my eyes. I do not mind at all . . . No I do not weep at the world, I am too busy sharpening my oyster knife."

2

A Paradise of My Own People

Chant another song of Harlem;
Not about the wrong of Harlem
But the worthy throng of Harlem,
Proud that they belong in Harlem;
They, the over-blamed of Harlem
Need not be ashamed of Harlem;
All is not ill-famed in Harlem
The devil, too, is tamed in Harlem.

—Anonymous

IN THE 1920S HARLEM centered on 135th Street and Seventh Avenue and reached from 110th Street to 150th Street. The area stretched from the East River to St. Nicholas Avenue on the west, a space of less than two square miles. Still, this small neighborhood, known as Black Manhattan, was also hailed as "the city of refuge" and the "Negro Mecca." To be in any part of Harlem during that period—to live there, to write or sing there, to dance there, even to visit there—was an immeasurable thrill. Better to "be a lamppost in Harlem than Governor of Georgia," as one popular saying described it.

A typical Harlem street scene in the 1920s. After Philip A. Payton and other black realtors began buying property in the area and selling and renting to blacks, Harlem became the neighborhood of choice for New York's African Americans.

Belongings packed, a share-cropper family prepares to leave its home for the long journey north.

Harlem was established in 1658 by Dutch settlers, who called it Nieuw Haarlem, after the city in Holland. It was a rural area until the 19th century, when improvements in transportation made it more accessible to lower Manhattan. Gradually, it became a fashionable residential community of New York City.

The Harlem Renaissance was in many ways the result of the Great Migration. Between 1900 and 1930, nearly three million African Americans left the South to seek their fortunes in the North, sending the black population of the North soaring by 400 percent. Although African Americans had been moving north since the time of the Civil War, the largest migration boom occurred around World War I, when nearly half a million rural blacks left the South in search of racial equality and greater economic opportunity.

Thanks to these migrants, New York's black neighborhoods grew more and more crowded. At the same time, in the middle-class white district of Harlem, real estate speculators were driving up property prices far beyond their actual value. The bubble burst around 1910. As prices plummeted, Harlem building owners panicked.

At this point, a number of black realtors also entered the volatile Harlem scene. Among them was Philip A. Payton Jr., who, along with other fast-moving entrepreneurs, knew that he could make large profits by opening this desirable neighborhood to blacks. He established the Afro-American Realty Company, leased or bought several Harlem buildings, and began renting to blacks. His move accelerated the local real estate panic; the remaining white property owners, certain that the presence of blacks would permanently depress prices, sold for whatever prices they could get and fled the neighborhood.

Of course, so many sellers brought still lower property prices, and black realtors began snapping up even more bargains. Ironically, the white landlords who stayed in Harlem began renting to blacks and made out very well. Prejudice and custom sharply limited the neighborhoods available to blacks, and Harlem was by far the best one open to them. For this reason, landlords could bring in rents proportionately higher than those paid by whites, who had many more choices. However, not all white landlords were pleased by this situation. "We have endeavored for some time to avoid turning over this house to colored tenants," remarked one white nonresident owner in 1916, "but as a result of . . . rapid changes in conditions . . . this issue has been forced upon us."

Many observers, including photographer Jacob Riis, also noted another irony: despite their protests, many white landlords favored African-

American tenants over what they referred to as the "lower grades of foreign people"—recently arrived European immigrants who, like the millions of blacks who moved north, were searching for greater economic opportunities than they had in their native countries.

Harlem's whites did not surrender the neighborhood without a fight. The president of the Harlem Property Owners Protective Association led the attack, discouraging Harlem land holders from selling or renting to African Americans and even offering to build a 24-foot-high fence at 136th Street to keep blacks out of the neighborhood. A local newspaper, the *Harlem Home News*, shrilly announced in July 1911 that white homeowners "must wake up and get busy before it is too late to repel the black hordes that stand ready to destroy the homes and scatter the fortunes of the whites living and doing business in the very heart of Harlem."

By that time, though, Harlem was already the neighborhood of choice for New York's African Americans. St. Philip's, New York's major black church, followed its parishioners to Harlem and bought up choice pieces of property. Black newspapers moved their offices to Harlem, too, as did African-American social clubs and political organizations. Thus was born *the* Harlem, a city within a city.

Realtor Philip Payton was not the only black millionaire in Harlem during this era. Like Madame C. J. Walker, he was among a number of African-American entrepreneurs who prospered by providing services and opportunities denied to African Americans by white-owned establishments.

Another was a woman known as "Pig Foot Mary." A "huge Goliath of a woman" according to one account, Lillian Harris arrived in New York in 1901 and took over a corner of the sidewalk of 60th Street, where she sold from a baby carriage southern delicacies like chitterlings, corn, hog-maw, and pig's feet—with the help of a nearby saloon owner who allowed her to use his stove. Displaced southern blacks were delighted to find such down-home fare in New York City, and Pig Foot Mary soon replaced her baby carriage with a steam table. In 1917 she moved to 135th Street and Lenox Avenue in Harlem where, as Mrs. John Dean, Pig Foot Mary purchased several buildings in Harlem and in Pasadena, California. By 1925, she was believed to own $325,000 in property. Legend has it that when her tenants' rent payments were overdue, they would receive a terse notice from their landlady: "Send it," she would write, "and send it damn quick."

By 1910, less than 25 percent of the more than 60,000 blacks who lived in Manhattan had been born in New York. The majority of the remaining blacks had come from rural or non-urban areas of the South. As a result, Harlem, like other predominantly African-American neighborhoods in the city, developed a decidedly southern, small-town flavor. Neighborhood churches flourished side-by-side with nightclubs—or "juke joints," as they were called in the South. Many of the same residents who would stay out celebrating on Saturday nights would spend their Sundays praising God in church services. Somehow, in Harlem, the two activities did not seem incompatible.

After church on Sunday, black Harlemites of all stripes—local barbers, city councilmen, jazz musicians, Broadway actresses—would stroll up and down Seventh Avenue between 125th and 138th Streets. "Indeed even Fifth Avenue on Easter never quite attains this," marveled physician and novelist Rudolph Fisher, referring to the traditional downtown spring "parade" of finery. "Practice makes perfect and Harlem's Seventh Avenue boasts fifty-two Easters a year."

Still, Harlem—indeed, the United States

Protesting the government's failure to control the East St. Louis riots, African Americans march in silent protest up New York City's Fifth Avenue. At least 30,000 people participated, including W. E. B. Du Bois, shown third from the right in the second row.

itself—was no paradise for African Americans. The years preceding the Harlem Renaissance had been rife with racial tension and violence. When the United States became involved in World War I in 1917, President Woodrow Wilson declared that America had entered the war to "make the world safe for democracy." Many African Americans thought his assertion hypocritical at best: although more than two million blacks registered for the wartime draft and 367,000 of them ultimately served, blacks living in the democratic United States had always been denied basic human rights.

In July 1917, only weeks after the United States entered the war, the black ghetto of East St. Louis, Illinois, witnessed one of the worst race riots the country had ever seen. After a group of whites drove through the neighborhood spraying gunfire into black homes, angry blacks shot and killed two policemen whom they mistakenly believed to be the perpetrators. In the ensuing riot, whites burned down the homes of blacks and killed occupants who attempted to flee from the burning buildings. At least 39 people were hanged, clubbed, shot, or stabbed to death. A few weeks later, a similar series of hostile events precipitated a riot in Houston,

Texas, involving members of the all-black 24th
Infantry. Seventeen whites and two blacks were
killed; in the court martial that followed, 20 black
soldiers were condemned to death, four of them
without right of appeal.

Amid such horrors were also moments of glory.
On February 17, 1919, the all-black 15th Regiment
of the New York National Guard—dubbed "Hell
Fighters" by their French allies—marched up Fifth
Avenue into Harlem in a triumphant victory
parade. Still officially the 369th Infantry Regiment,
these men had been in continuous combat longer
than any other American unit. They were the only
unit in the war permitted to fly a state flag and the
only one awarded the Croix de Guerre, France's
most distinguished military honor. The 15th had
been the first Allied unit to reach the Rhine River
during the offensive attack on Germany.

Headed by Lieutenant James Reese "Big Jim"
Europe, the only African-American officer, the reg-
imental band led 18 white officers and 1,300 black
soldiers through New York City. A well-known
bandleader in prewar America, Europe had introduced the new sound of jazz overseas, sparking a
craze that drew dozens of American performers and
musicians abroad, including dancer Josephine
Baker in the 1920s and jazz greats Dizzy Gillespie,
Ella Fitzgerald, Lester Young, and Charlie Parker in
later decades.

When the 15th crossed 130th Street into
Harlem, the band burst into the swing tune "Here
Comes My Daddy." The crowd went wild. The soldiers, who had been marching in tight formation,
opened ranks in welcome. "We marched through
Harlem singing and laughing," Major Arthur Little
recalled. These soldiers were more than just symbols
of pride in Harlem. They were the brothers, sons,
and fathers of many of the area's residents. The men
of the 15th Regiment were home.

The legendary 369th Infantry Regiment thunders up Fifth Avenue into Harlem.

Race relations in America had continued to deteriorate. W. E. B. Du Bois, whose editorials in *The Crisis* profoundly influenced African Americans across the country, urged African Americans to respond to the situation with militance: "We return from the slavery of the uniform which the world's madness demanded us to don to the freedom of civil garb," he wrote. *"We return. We return from fighting. We return fighting.* Make way for Democracy! We saved it in France, and by the Great Jehovah, we will save it in the United States of America, or know the reason why."

White America had other ideas, however. Later that year, race riots broke out in two dozen cities across the United States, including Washington, D.C.; Chicago, Illinois; Longview, Texas; and Knoxville, Tennessee. More than 60 blacks were lynched in the steady stream of bloodshed that James Weldon Johnson would refer to as "the Red Summer."

The increase in racial violence was accompanied by a revival of the Ku Klux Klan. Founded in 1866, this dreaded white supremacist organization had won a large following in the South after the Civil War. The hooded and white-robed Klansmen launched terror attacks against blacks and fought to overturn the racial equality measures passed during Reconstruction. The Klan's resurgence began in Georgia in 1915, spurred in part by the vast waves of European immigrants entering America and the burgeoning black nationalist movement. By the 1920s its message of bigotry, violence, and bitter hatred of black people had expanded to include Jews, Catholics, atheists, immigrants, and anyone else considered racially or morally "impure." Blacks remained the Klan's favorite victims, though, and among the blacks specifically targeted were veterans returning from the battlefields of World War I. Their confidence strengthened by experience in war, black men with military training were by Klan standards nothing but trouble. Of the more than 70 blacks reported lynched in 1919, 10 were soldiers.

African Americans were outraged by the violence directed at them. They had enthusiastically supported the war effort, not only by enlisting in the armed services but by buying war bonds. But instead of greater freedom, they faced even worse oppression after the war. Du Bois launched a scathing indictment of the white establishment that was turning a blind eye to such violence. "No land that loves to lynch 'niggers' can lead the hosts of Almighty God," Du Bois raged.

Pushed to the wall, blacks began organizing anti-lynching campaigns in the hope that public horror might lead to legislation against the practice. The vigorous commitment of thousands of African Americans, including journalist Ida Wells-Barnett, educators Mary McLeod Bethune and Mary B. Talbert, and activists Alice Dunbar Nelson, Walter White, and W. E. B. Du Bois eventually had an effect. Between 1919 and 1923 an estimated 300 lynchings took place; between 1924 and 1928 the number dropped to 100. Contributing heavily to this decline were the educational efforts of the Anti-Lynching Crusaders (led by Talbert) and the NAACP, both of which publicized photographs, eyewitness reports, and statistics that demonstrated the viciousness of the crime.

In this explosive atmosphere, white America's appreciation of black culture rarely extended past the entrances of cabarets and theaters. Although African-American performers had long since moved from vaudeville houses to Broadway (the first African-American production to reach Broadway was John W. Isham's *Oriental America* in 1896), the commonly held view of blacks as unequal to whites in intelligence and sophistication remained evident even there. "Ecstasy seems to be [the black's] natural state," wrote white critic Joseph Wood Krutch of black entertainers.

For this reason, black intellectuals such as Du Bois did not always agree with the trends of the Harlem Renaissance. The popular music and entertainment that brought crowds of whites into Harlem were to Du Bois not much better than the minstrel shows of the late 19th century, filled with blackfaced performers acting in melodramas whose themes revolved around black inferiority. Early in the movement, Du Bois criticized black artists for producing works that functioned chiefly as racial propaganda. It was important, he maintained, for artists to present the world as they found it.

However, by the middle of the decade, he felt that some artists, especially the writer Claude McKay, had gone too far in portraying both the destitution and the caged desires of black men and women. Du Bois feared that such exaggerated writings would substantiate the false notions that whites held about black life. Out of the belief that black art

should elevate the race, Du Bois published his second novel, *Dark Princess*, in 1928.

Meanwhile, the "New Negroes," as Howard University professor Alain Locke called the younger black writers of the movement, believed that a deliberately sunny view of black life was artistically dishonest. Langston Hughes, writing for *The Nation* magazine in a 1926 article entitled "The Negro Artist and the Racial Mountain," declared:

> We younger Negro artists who create now intend to express our individual dark-skinned selves without fear or shame. If white people are pleased, we are glad. If they are not, it doesn't matter. We know we are beautiful. And ugly too. If colored people are pleased, we are glad. If they are not, their displeasure doesn't matter either.

However, the displeasure of the literary blacks of Harlem could be quite forceful.

3

The Talented Tenth

IN HIS 1940 AUTOBIOGRAPHY, *The Big Sea*, Langston Hughes noted that his 1927 poetry collection, *Fine Clothes to the Jew*, which dealt with the seedy side of Harlem life, prompted headlines in the black press that read "LANGSTON HUGHES' BOOK OF POEMS TRASH" and "LANGSTON HUGHES—THE SEWER DWELLER."

Like Hughes, another young black writer, Jamaican-born Claude McKay, was not the sort of writer who feared such controversy. At 23, already the author of two volumes of dialect poetry, McKay traveled to America to study agriculture. As a student at Kansas State College, he read Du Bois's *The Souls of Black Folk*, a collection of sketches and essays published in 1903. The book shook him "like an earthquake"; soon after, he decided to make a career out of writing poetry and arrived in Harlem in 1914.

Deeply troubled by American racist violence and the terror of the Red Summer of 1919, he wrote the poem, "If We Must Die," a militant call for self-defense. The poem reads in part:

One of America's principal black intellectuals, W. E. B. Du Bois emerged as the leading voice in the struggle for racial advancement during the first half of the 20th century.

If we must die, let it not be like hogs
Hunted and penned in an inglorious spot,
While round us bark the mad and hungry dogs,
Making their mock at our accursed lot. . . .
Like men, we'll face the murderous, cowardly pack,
Pressed to the wall, dying but fighting back!

The bold fury and racial pride of the poem made it an anthem for African Americans. Along with his first book of poetry, *Harlem Shadows* (1922), "If We Must Die" transformed McKay into the first literary star of the Harlem Renaissance. "No Negro poet has sung more beautifully of his race than McKay," James Weldon Johnson said in a New York *Age* review, "and no poet has ever equaled the power with which he expresses the bitterness that so often rises in the heart of the race."

A restless character, uneasy with success yet hungry for it, McKay was never completely comfortable in Harlem. Most whites outside the area viewed him as just another black man, yet he did not feel at ease with members of the black intellectual circle. He left New York in 1922 for the Soviet Union so that he could witness communism firsthand, and later he moved to France. Although he was overseas during most of the Harlem Renaissance, he continued to write about Harlem. "I had done my best Harlem stuff when I was abroad, seeing it from a long perspective," he later claimed in *A Long Way from Home.*

McKay eventually returned to Harlem, however. After years of travel and life abroad, the "Negro Mecca" would lure him home again. "Harlem was my first positive reaction to American life," he once said. "It was like entering a paradise of my own people."

McKay was one of the many young writers of the Harlem Renaissance who was strongly influenced by W. E. B. Du Bois, one of the most important black intellectual figures of the 20th century. "My earliest

Booker T. Washington at the Tuskegee Institute, 1902, with secretary Emmett Scott. Although Du Bois agreed with Washington's emphasis on economic growth for blacks, he did not agree with Washington that blacks should put off agitating for equal rights.

memories of written words were those of W. E. B. Du Bois and the Bible," Langston Hughes recalled.

Du Bois was born and raised in the small town of Great Barrington, Massachusetts. Of mixed heritage—Dutch, French, and African American—Du Bois was light-skinned and relatively sheltered from prejudice. He graduated from high school in 1884, the only black in his class and the first ever to graduate from the school. His ultimate goal was to attend Harvard College, widely regarded as one of the best schools in the country, but Harvard turned down his application for admission. Enthusiastic townspeople, including the high school principal and two ministers, set up a scholarship fund for Du Bois and sent him instead to Fisk University in Nashville, Tennessee, a school for blacks that aimed to become one of the best educational institutions in the South.

Though deeply disappointed that he could not attend Harvard, the young scholar was eager to journey to the South to "meet colored people of my own age and education, of my own ambitions." Southern blacks lived in a segregated society, where they could not vote or hold public office, and Du Bois felt that if he wanted to be a leader of his people, he would have to begin there.

Du Bois eventually did attend Harvard, earning a Ph.D. in 1896. By this time, he had been exposed to the brutality of racial prejudice and the nearly inescapable poverty of many southern blacks. Working among the rural poor of the South had inflamed his social conscience, and he grew committed to helping his fellow blacks to lift "the Veil that hung between us and Opportunity." In his third year at Fisk, he had announced in an editorial that he was devoting himself "toward a life that shall be an honor to the Race."

Du Bois's brilliance was matched by his pride and ambition. Dogged in his efforts to refute those who doubted "Negro intelligence" and who had initially denied him a place at Harvard, Du Bois studied economics at the University of Berlin in Germany. "The problem of the twentieth century is the problem of the color line," he wrote in *The Souls of Black Folk*.

Du Bois's vision of black leadership was at heart decidedly elitist. He firmly believed that educated blacks—the small percentage of black intellectuals to whom he referred as the "Talented Tenth"—should provide the strong leadership that the nation's blacks so desperately needed. "The Negro race, like all races, is going to be saved by its exceptional men," he wrote. Du Bois insisted that middle-class blacks use their advanced knowledge of modern culture to lead the struggle for black rights. The

Talented Tenth theory, which grew out of the con-
clusions Du Bois had reached in his study *The
Philadelphia Negro*, seemed to him the only way to
supplant white leadership.

Despite the Harvard education that separated
him from the vast majority of African Americans,
Du Bois's work appealed to a wide audience, from
northern liberals to rural blacks in the South. Under
his editorship, the NAACP's *The Crisis* reached a
monthly circulation of almost 100,000 copies.

Du Bois's philosophy was in direct opposition to
that of another black leader, Booker T. Washington,
a former slave and founder of the Tuskegee Normal
and Industrial Institute for Blacks. Washington held
that the way to raise blacks up was to supply job
training for them.

Speaking before an audience of blacks and
whites at the 1895 Cotton States and International
Exposition in Atlanta, Washington exhorted blacks
to put aside their aspirations for political and social
equality and strive instead to improve their industrial skills before demanding a higher place in
American society. In the speech, which Du Bois
would call the "Atlanta Compromise," Washington
maintained that the "wisest among my race under-
stand that the agitation of questions of social equality is the extremest folly." Once blacks had made a
substantial economic contribution to the nation,
social and political equality would follow.

Although Du Bois initially sympathized with
Washington—*The Philadelphia Negro* had also promoted the virtues of thrift and self-reliance as
solutions to the problems faced by blacks—he
increasingly began to believe that Washington had
contributed significantly to worsening racial relations in the United States. Du Bois was not the only
influential black who disagreed vigorously with
Washington. Among others were journalists Ida
Wells-Barnett and William Monroe Trotter, who

Although The Brownies'
Book, *a monthly for young
black readers, lasted for only
two years, Du Bois looked
back on the project "with infi-
nite satisfaction."*

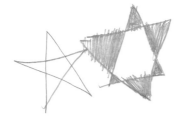

felt that Washington's views were a betrayal of their civil rights.

Du Bois contributed to the Harlem Renaissance in many ways besides his work with *The Crisis*. An annual feature of the periodical was a special children's edition, and in early 1920, with the help of coeditors Jessie Fauset and Augustus Dill, he began publishing another magazine: *The Brownies' Book*, a monthly that included stories, poems, and short biographies aimed at a young black audience. Du Bois, who professed a great love for children, appeared in each issue as a character named the Crow. "I like my black feathers—don't you?" his alter ego asked of his youthful readers.

Many of the young writers of the Harlem Renaissance fit neatly into Du Bois's vision of a black "aristocracy" that would lead other African Americans to equality. It was the literary editor of *The Crisis*, a fiercely intelligent woman named Jessie Fauset, who would be the first to herald the talent of such important Renaissance writers as Claude McKay, Jean Toomer, Countee Cullen, and Langston Hughes.

The independent and intellectually brilliant Fauset was 37 years old when the literary world began paying attention to what Harlemites had to say. She had earned a degree in classical languages from Cornell University in 1905, after which she taught French for 14 years at Washington's Paul Laurence Dunbar High School, where many of the children of the city's black elite were enrolled. (Fauset had hoped to attend Bryn Mawr College, a prestigious women's school in Pennsylvania, but after accepting her application, Bryn Mawr offered to find her a scholarship elsewhere lest she start a wave of integration.) A traditional classicist and Europhile, Fauset traveled to Europe repeatedly before earning a master's degree in French from the University of Pennsylvania in 1919.

Some of her students later noted that Fauset never seemed to be fully satisfied as a teacher and always imagined herself going on to greater things. She was very aware, however, of the double yoke of gender and race bias placed upon her. "Had she not been a 'colored woman' she might have sought work with a New York publishing house," David Levering Lewis wrote in *When Harlem Was in Vogue*. "There is no telling what she would have done had she been a man, given her first-rate mind and formidable efficiency at any task." Through her relationship

Du Bois at work on The Crisis, *with coeditors Jessie Fauset (left) and Augustus Dill (standing) in the editorial offices. Du Bois was the main voice of* The Crisis *for 24 years.*

with Du Bois, which had begun while she was attending Cornell, Fauset secured a position as literary editor for *The Crisis* in 1919.

Seven years earlier, a Florida native named James Weldon Johnson had published *The Autobiography of an Ex-Colored Man*, a novel about a light-skinned black man trying to pass as a white. Although it received little critical attention, it influenced a number of young black artists of the Harlem Renaissance who were rebelling against a white society at the same time that they were depending on white patrons and white readers to support their creative work.

The son of the first black female teacher in the state of Florida, Johnson was educated at Atlanta University and followed in his mother's footsteps as a director of a high school for African Americans. He edited a small newspaper, studied law, and was admitted to the Florida bar. Johnson had been appointed United States consul to Venezuela and Nicaragua and was field secretary of the NAACP before being named the organization's executive secretary in 1920.

As a columnist for the New York Age, Johnson called attention to many outstanding young black writers. In 1922, he brought them further notice when he published The Book of American Negro Poetry, an anthology of poems by 40 talented black writers, beginning with Paul Laurence Dunbar and ending with Claude McKay. In his introduction to the book, Johnson traced the history of black poetry from its early writers, such as the 18th-century poet Phillis Wheatley, to its dialect poets, such as Dunbar. He stated that the artistic achievements of black Americans had been limited because "the Negro in the United States is consuming all of his intellectual energy in this grueling race struggle."

A former protégé of Booker T. Washington, Johnson also believed in Du Bois's notion of a Talented Tenth. He valued the rich tradition of African-American spirituals, slave songs, and biblical stories, yet he believed that those who had the power to effect social change were the high-minded, scholarly men and women of society. Johnson wrote in his introduction:

> The final measure of the greatness of all peoples is the amount and standard of the literature and art they have produced. The world does not know that a people is great until that people produces great literature and art. . . . And nothing will do more to change the mental attitude and raise his status than a demonstration of the intellectual parity by the Negro through the production of literature and art.

Another of the six "midwives" of the Harlem Renaissance (with Jessie Fauset, James Weldon Johnson, Charles S. Johnson, Casper Holstein, and

Walter White) was Alain Locke. A Phi Beta Kappa Harvard graduate and the first black American to win a Rhodes scholarship to Oxford University in England, Alain Locke was the epitome of Du Bois's Talented Tenth. He came from a well-educated and ambitious family; his mother, from whom he acquired his love of literature, taught at Philadelphia's Institute for Colored Youth. After receiving his degree from Oxford, Locke studied for a year at the University of Berlin and for another year at the Collège de France. He returned to America in 1912, having cultivated an image that he would keep throughout his life—a high-pitched, affected way of speaking, impeccably tailored suits, and a thin umbrella that he used as a walking stick.

Locke became a professor of philosophy at Howard University. With dramatic arts instructor Montgomery Gregory, Locke sought to bring the spirit of the Harlem Renaissance, with its pride in black America's cultural heritage, to the relatively staid Howard community. The two sponsored a campus literary club called Stylus, whose membership included Zora Neale Hurston. Hurston's first short story, "John Redding Goes to Sea," appeared in the May 1921 issue of the club's literary magazine. "We now have enough talent," Locke wrote at the time, "to begin a movement and to express a school of thought."

Locke was anxious to foster in his students an appreciation of the African art and European literature that he loved, but he was often criticized for his haughty demeanor. Hurston once described him as the "one who lives by quotations trying to criticize people who live by life." Locke believed, however, that such disapproval was the price one paid for cultural literacy: "the highest intellectual duty is the duty to be cultured," he told his students. They should ignore "criticism of exclusiveness, over-selectness, perhaps even the extreme of snobbery.

Author, editor, and NAACP chief James Weldon Johnson firmly believed that African Americans could rise only through the arts. "The final measure of the greatness of all peoples," he said, "is the amount and standard of the literature and art they have produced."

Culture will have to plead guilty to a certain degree of this." With his close ties to Charlotte Osgood Mason, a white patron of the Harlem Renaissance, and despite—or perhaps because of—his air of superiority, Locke was an enormously influential mentor for striving black artists, musicians, and writers in Harlem.

4

Home to Harlem

UNLIKE ALAIN LOCKE, Jean Toomer was not a paradigm of the Talented Tenth. The ambitious Washington-born writer first caused a stir in 1922 with the publication of his poems in the New Orleans magazine *Double-Dealer* and in *Secession S4N*—and eventually in *The Liberator*, whose editor, Claude McKay, had initially rejected "Miss Toomer's" work. "Where did you get a chance to work out your technique?" an enthusiastic Jessie Fauset wrote him.

Novelist and short-story writer Sherwood Anderson declared Toomer's the "first negro work I have seen that strikes me as really new." The two authors began corresponding regularly. Toomer wrote that he believed Anderson strived in his work to present "the beauty that the Negro has in him," while Anderson worried that Toomer's unsophisticated style would be spoiled by white acclaim. However, when Toomer's remarkable novel *Cane* appeared in 1923, Anderson wrote that he had "plunged into it and finished it" in one sitting. "It dances," he exclaimed.

Although *Cane* would become one of the liter-

An extended southern family prepares for a Sunday afternoon of hymn singing. Toomer was captivated by the "strangely rich and beautiful" folk songs and spirituals he heard while working among blacks in the rural South.

ary cornerstones of the Harlem Renaissance, its author was atypical of the movement's members. Unlike McKay, whose racial pride ran deep, Toomer's relationship with the black community was ambiguous at best. Nathan Eugene Toomer grew up in an affluent white neighborhood of Washington, D.C., with his grandfather, Pinckney Benton Stewart Pinchback, a former United States senator. He later described his family as belonging to "an aristocracy—such as never existed before and perhaps never will exist again in America—midway between the white and negro worlds." His white mother, who had married the mulatto son of a white North Carolina landowner, remarried after Nathan Toomer left her and moved to Brooklyn. After her death, Jean moved with his grandparents to a black neighborhood in Washington—his first experience living among African Americans.

Throughout his life, Toomer would have mixed feelings about his racial heritage. Muscular and handsome with dark eyes and thick, wavy hair, Toomer also had very fair skin, which allowed him to pass as white. He would later deny that he was of black ancestry at all. "When I live with blacks, I'm Negro," Toomer later said. "When I live with the whites, I'm white, or better, a foreigner. I used to puzzle my own brain with the question. But now I'm done with it."

After briefly attending the University of Wisconsin and the Massachusetts College of Agriculture, Toomer ended up in Chicago at the American College of Physical Training. There he became drawn to the study of sociology; he moved to New York and attended City College and New York University. Still restless, he tried and failed to enter the army, sold cars, taught physical education, and traveled by rail and by hitchhiking before beginning to write in earnest. Finally, at a literary party in New York, he discovered people who he felt were like him. "Here was the first gathering of people I had ever seen in my life—people who were of my kind. It was simply a matter of learning to speak their language."

Soon after, Toomer had an experience of a different sort. In 1921, he volunteered to run a small agricultural and industrial school in Sparta, Georgia. What he witnessed in the rural South, the "strangely rich and beautiful" world of folk songs and spirituals, transformed him. "God, but they feel the thing," he said of the music, "[a]lways sincerely, powerfully, deeply. And when they overflow in song, there is no singing that has so touched me." He would write to Sherwood Anderson a year later, "My seed was planted in *myself* down there. Roots have grown and strengthened."

This introduction to southern black culture

Countee Cullen, among the most renowned writers of the Harlem Renaissance, struggled against being typed as a "Negro poet." Yet his classic poetic style and spiritual subject matter greatly appealed to the black elite of Harlem.

resulted in Toomer's masterpiece, *Cane*. Amazed by the soul-rocking black spirituals, charmed by the sharecroppers and beautiful country women that he met, he wrote:

> O land and soil, red soil and sweet-gum tree,
> So scant of grass, so profligate of pines,
> Now just before an epoch's sun declines
> Thy son, in time, I have returned to thee,
> Thy son, I have in time returned to thee.
>
> In time, for though the sun is setting on
> A song-lit race of slaves, it has not set;
> Though late, O soil, it is not too late yet
> To catch thy plaintive soul, leaving, soon gone,
> Leaving, to catch thy plaintive soul soon gone.

Toomer divided his book into three parts: a series of vignettes of southern black women, a collection of literary sketches set in the urban landscapes of Washington and Chicago, and a free-form play set in Georgia. The literary world at the time was enamored of the brief, pointed observations of imagist poetry, which aimed not simply to describe images but to present them as whole pictures. Toomer's book—part poetry and part narrative, a montage of images that seem more like a painting or film than a book—strongly appealed to critics, and the author was hailed as a writer of rare ability. Boston critic William Stanley Braithwaite lauded the book as one "of gold and bronze, of dusk and flame, of ecstasy and pain" and the author as "a bright morning star of a new day of the race in literature."

Although the author and his publisher promised more works of the caliber of *Cane*, Toomer would write only one more lyrical work, the long poem "Blue Meridian," published in 1929. Shortly after *Cane* was published, Toomer met the Russian philosopher Georgi Ivanovitch Gurdjieff and was so taken with his ideas that he left for France to study under him. When he returned to Harlem in 1924, he had become a disciple, adopting Gurdjieff's teachings as eagerly as he had absorbed black southern culture. "I am not sure that I have a soul, but if I have, then Gurdjieff has penetrated the shell and written upon the kernel indelibly," he wrote.

Toomer moved increasingly into the white, bohemian circles of Greenwich Village, surrounding himself with cultural figures like Edmund Wilson, Marianne Moore, and Georgia O'Keefe. "So Jean Toomer shortly left his Harlem group and went downtown," said Langston Hughes with regret, and the "Negroes lost one of the most talented of all their writers."

There would be no such desertion of the African-American world by Countee Cullen. Graceful, brilliant, and gregarious, Cullen was also a natural poet and easily the best-known Harlem writer of the 1920s. The Harlem establishment much preferred his subject matter—often African-American spirituality—to Claude McKay's radicalism or Langston Hughes's street scenes.

Cullen was first published when he was 15. Prodigiously talented, he won nearly every poetry prize available to students. By the time he graduated from New York University in 1925, he was being published regularly. His first collection, *Color*, appeared to great critical acclaim in 1925. Cullen received a master of arts degree from Harvard University and began working as an assistant editor for *Opportunity* the next year. In 1927, he published two poetry collections, *Copper Sun* and *The Ballad of the Brown Girl*, and edited an anthology of black poetry, *Caroling Dusk*.

Cullen is a somewhat mysterious figure to biographers because he lied freely about his background and definitive records of his childhood have never been found. He was probably born in Louisville, Kentucky, in 1903. Apparently abandoned by his father, he was taken by his mother to Baltimore to live with his paternal grandmother. As a teenager he moved to Harlem, where Carolyn Cullen and her husband, the Reverend Frederick Cullen, adopted him. Countee's adoptive father was pastor of Harlem's Salem Methodist Episcopal Church, which had approximately 2,500 members by the mid-1920s. A respected community leader, Frederick Cullen was also a long-standing member of the NAACP.

Cullen's birth mother lived in Louisville until her death in 1940. Although Countee regularly sent money to her, he seems never to have recovered from the sting of her abandonment, as reflected in much of his work. Despite this apparent "dark side," Cullen's impeccable manners and solicitous demeanor helped to make him popular in Harlem, and his writing captured the pride and the spirit of Harlem's creative explosion in a way that no one else's could. In his poem "Harlem Wine" he wrote:

> This is not water running here,
> These thick rebellious streams
> That hurtle flesh and bone past fear
> Down alleyways of dreams.
>
> This is a wine that must flow on
> Not caring how or where,
> So it has ways to flow upon
> Where song is in the air.
>
> So it can woo an artful flute
> With loose, elastic lips,
> Its measurement of joy compute
> With blithe, ecstatic hips.

Cullen married Yolande Du Bois, the daughter of W. E. B. Du Bois, in an elaborate celebration in April 1928, but the marriage lasted less than a year. His last poetry collection, *The Black Christ and Other Poems*, was published in 1929. He later wrote children's books and a novel.

If the flamboyant Zora Neale Hurston was

the self-appointed "wild child" of the Harlem Renaissance, then Langston Hughes was its golden boy. When first introduced to Hughes, W. E. B. Du Bois was uncharacteristically warm to the young poet, and at their first meeting, the usually formal Jessie Fauset, with whom Hughes had corresponded, extended an invitation for him to visit her home. When Hughes hesitated, she touched his shoulder in reassurance. "I mean this," she said, "because I feel that we are genuinely indebted to you at [*The Crisis*]."

"You will like him, I love him," Countee Cullen wrote to Alain Locke after meeting Hughes, to whom he later dedicated his poem "To a Brown Boy." Perhaps so great an affection from such dissimilar sources was not surprising: Hughes arrived in Harlem with an open heart. "There is no thrill in all the world," he said, "like entering, for the first time, New York harbor. . . . New York is truly the dream city." And of his new neighborhood, he confessed, "I was in love with Harlem long before I got here."

Born in Joplin, Missouri, in 1902, Hughes never had a stable family life. His mother's uncle had been dean of Howard University's Law School, a U.S. Ambassador to Haiti, and a Virginia congressman in 1888, and his maternal grandmother was the first African-American woman to graduate from Oberlin College. Hughes's parents, though, had a tempestuous relationship, and the child was constantly shuffled from Mexico, where his father had moved the family, to Missouri, Kansas, and Illinois.

Lonely and never feeling truly at home, Hughes found early solace in literature, devouring the work of such poets as Amy Lowell, Carl Sandburg, and Walt Whitman. According to his 1940 autobiography, *The Big Sea*, he began to "believe in nothing but books, and the wonderful world in books—where if people suffered, they suffered in beautiful

"I was in love with Harlem long before I got here," Hughes said of the neighborhood that became his home. Though he often suggested that he felt isolated from others, he was regarded by those who knew him as full of warmth and joy.

Black patrons enjoy themselves in a Harlem nightclub in the 1930s. In poems like "The Weary Blues," Hughes captured with remarkable accuracy the everyday experiences and the musical and spoken cadences of African Americans.

language, not [in] monosyllables, as we did in Kansas." He spent his high school years in Cleveland, sustained by his books, poetry, and charming personality.

Hughes's words attracted Harlem's notice long before he arrived there himself. Aboard a train to Mexico in 1920, Hughes crossed the Mississippi River and began writing a poem that would become his celebrated "The Negro Speaks of Rivers."

> I've known rivers:
> I've known rivers ancient as the world and older
>   than the flow of human blood in human veins.
>
> My soul has grown deep like the rivers.
>
> I bathed in the Euphrates when dawns were young.

I built my hut near the Congo and it lulled me to
    sleep.
I looked upon the Nile and raised the pyramids
    above it.
I heard the singing of the Mississippi
    when Abe Lincoln
went down to New Orleans, and I've seen its muddy
    bosom turn all golden in the sunset.

I've known rivers:
Ancient, dusky rivers.

My soul has grown deep like the rivers.

The 19-year-old poet sent his work to Jessie Fauset,
and in the March 1926 issue of *The Crisis*, Fauset
wrote that she "took [Hughes's] beautiful dignified
creation to Dr. Du Bois" and asked him, "What colored person is there . . . in the United States who
writes like that and yet is unknown to us?"

The next year Hughes arrived in New York,
purportedly to study mining at Columbia University but, according to *The Big Sea*, "mainly because
[he] wanted to see Harlem." He was promptly ush-
ered into the literary scene, where he was introduced to numerous critics and writers. Not surprisingly, he spent more time attending plays, concerts,
lectures, and literary debates than studying. He left
Columbia in 1922.

Hughes spent a great deal of time during his first
year in New York at the Harlem branch of the New
York Public Library. One of the people he met there
was Countee Cullen. The two men got along well
and traded poems with one another for appraisal
and criticism.

Cullen and Hughes approached their poetry in
different ways. Cullen wrote poetry that demanded
exact syllable counts and certain sounds to complete
a rhyme scheme. Hughes, on the other hand, preferred to write in free verse. Like Cullen, he careful-
ly chose his language to fit the subject and emotion

of his poems, but his poetry was less formal in style.

The two poets also held differing views about the relationship between their race and their poetry. Hughes could not separate his interest in blacks from his desire to write poetry. He wrote about black people, black music, and black experiences while using African-American speech rhythms and slang. Cullen considered himself a poet first—one who just happened to be black—so he did not center his poetry on blackness. Instead, he tended to write in a private voice about personal matters. In this way, he was almost the opposite of Hughes, who wrote in a boisterous voice about public events: lynchings, jazz clubs, bill collectors, and the like. Despite these differences, the two men encouraged each other's work. Cullen even read some of Hughes's poems in public readings at the library.

Hughes's writing career was launched in 1925 when "The Weary Blues" won the *Opportunity* magazine contest. The poem, which reveals the loneliness Hughes was feeling, also captures the cadences of black music and speech. It reads in part:

> Droning on a drowsy syncopated tune,
> Rocking back and forth to a mellow croon,
>   I heard a Negro play.
> Down on Lenox Avenue the other night
> By the pale dull pallor of an old gas light
>   He did a lazy sway. . . .
>   He did a lazy sway. . . .
> To the tune o' those Weary Blues.
> With his ebony hands on each ivory key
> He made the poor piano moan with melody.
>   O Blues!
> Swaying to and fro on his rickety stool
> He played that sad raggy tune like a musical fool.
>   Sweet Blues!
> Coming from a black man's soul.
>   O Blues!. . . .
>
> And far into the night he crooned that tune.
> The stars went out and so did the moon.

The singer stopped playing and went to bed
While the Weary Blues echoed through his head.
He slept like a rock or a man that's dead.

What Hughes accomplished in this poem was new and remarkable. His use of rhythm, imitating black speech and blues music, was a brilliant coup. In writing the poem, he took the sounds of street music and talk and transformed them into a powerful and evocative voice all his own.

Although Hughes would travel to Africa, the Netherlands, France, Cuba, Haiti, and the Soviet Union and throughout the United States, the young poet who grew up lonely and unsure of his place in the world had found more than success and acclaim in Harlem—he had found a home and a way of expressing himself as an African American. His friend Arna Bontemps would describe Hughes's appreciation for black culture in a 1952 *Saturday Review* article: "Few people have enjoyed being Negro as much as Langston Hughes," Bontemps wrote. "He would not have missed the experience of being what he is for the world."

5

Renaissance Women

IN 1770, A BOSTON slave named Phillis Wheatley published *An Elegaic Poem, on the Death of that Celebrated Divine, and Eminent Servant of Jesus Christ, the Reverend and Learned George Whitefield.* Wheatley's work received high praise from many whites—who had not believed that it was possible to educate slaves. However, Wheatley was schooled in the classics and in English literature; she knew the Bible and had learned Latin. Although she did not address the position of her race in colonial American society, she was keenly aware of political events, as is evident in her many poetic appeals to such men as King George III, the Earl of Dartmouth, and George Washington.

Wheatley is one of the first of many African-American women whose contributions to art and literature have been largely unacknowledged. Another is civil rights leader and poet Frances Ellen Watkins Harper. Born around 1825 in the slave state of Maryland to free parents, Harper published her first volume of poetry, *Forest Leaves*, when she was 20 years old. Later, as a professional abolitionist, she traveled across the country, lecturing and read-

Augusta Savage with her sculpture Realization *(1934). Savage was one of the few members of the Harlem Renaissance to remain in Harlem after the movement's demise, founding her own art school and becoming the first black member of the National Association for Women Painters and Sculptors.*

ing her poems. Her only novel, *Iola Leroy; or, Shadows Uplifted* (1892), which relates the story of a mulatto and her family during and after the Civil War, has only recently attracted critical attention.

Eight years after *Iola Leroy* appeared, another black woman, Pauline E. Hopkins, published a novel about the relationship between a mulatto man and an octoroon woman: *Contending Forces: A Romance Illustrative of Negro Life North and South* (1900). Hopkins wrote three more novels about the lives of black women within white society, but her work went mostly unnoticed until the 1970s, when *Contending Forces* was hailed as a pioneering work of African-American fiction.

The Harlem Renaissance could not have happened without the invaluable contributions of women writers and artists. The drama and irreverence of Zora Neale Hurston, the intellectual brilliance of Jessie Fauset, the iconoclastic themes of Nella Larsen, and the talent and enthusiasm of artists Gwendolyn Bennett and Augusta Savage were essential to the development of the distinct African-American artistic voice that grew out of the Harlem Renaissance.

"All you had to say was 580," said Ethel Ray Nance, Charles Johnson's secretary. "They knew you meant 580 St. Nicholas [Avenue]." It was common knowledge that when one arrived in Harlem in the 1920s, the apartment Nance shared with Regina Anderson, Louella Tucker, and tenant Ethel Waters was one of the first places to go. Part of a luxurious complex situated in Sugar Hill, the most affluent section of Harlem, the apartment functioned as a welcoming suite for newcomers to the area.

The women of 580 served as tour guides and hostesses for the black literary circle, including Langston Hughes, Jean Toomer, essayist Eric Walrond, and painter Aaron Douglas. To celebrate

Jessie Fauset (left), Langston Hughes (center), and Zora Neale Hurston meet near a statue of Booker T. Washington during a 1927 visit to Alabama's Tuskegee Institute, founded by Washington.

Countee Cullen's graduation from college, for example, Nance and her friends took the genteel young poet to his first nightclub, a Fifth Avenue basement club called The Cat on the Saxophone.

When she arrived in Harlem in January 1925, Zora Neale Hurston had already earned fame for her short story "Drenched in Light," which had appeared in the December 1924 issue of *Opportunity*. A literary celebrity within months of her arrival (she won two *Opportunity* awards for her play *Color Struck* and her short story "Spunk"), Hurston found herself sought out by New York's artistic community, including the eminent black writers Jessie Fauset, Arna Bontemps, Eric Walrond, and Bruce

Nugent. She was also befriended by many of the city's white writers, artists, and patrons of the arts. Popular novelist Fannie Hurst, humorist Irvin S. Cobb, and movie mogul Jesse Lasky were among the wealthy whites who invited her to dinner parties and nightclubs.

Born and bred in the rural South, Hurston sometimes spoke with an earthiness that shocked her associates, many of them blacks with middle-class sensibilities. For this reason, Charles Johnson asked Ethel Nance to watch out for the outrageous and headstrong Hurston. She had attracted the attention of another influential admirer: writer Annie Nathan Meyer, a founder of Barnard, the undergraduate college for women of Columbia University, and Johnson was concerned that Hurston would not keep her appointments or attend the many conferences required for admission. "[W]ith her," explained Nance, "if something else interesting came up, she was off."

Hurston won a scholarship and accepted Fannie Hurst's invitation to become her live-in secretary. Mystified by filing and unable to type or take shorthand, Hurston proved a disaster as a secretary. She and Hurst became good friends, however, and the young writer stayed on as the novelist's chauffer, companion, and, Hurston hinted to friends, her prize pet. The Negro, it was often said, was "in vogue," and Zora Neale Hurston always attracted attention.

Hurston was indeed a colorful figure, sporting a turban in imitation of an Indian princess when driving Hurst to appointments. Her talent for storytelling was legendary, but the young author's flamboyance also drew criticism. Some Harlemites accused her of pandering to white stereotypes about blacks. "She was always getting scholarships and things from wealthy white people," Langston Hughes remarked, "some of whom simply paid her just to

(continued on page 73)

Treasures of Harlem

Church on Lenox Avenue,
William H. Johnson,
ca. 1939-40
(color photo 1)

Street Life, Harlem,
William H. Johnson,
ca. 1939-40
(color photo 2)

Jitterbugs (III),
William H. Johnson,
ca. 1941
(color photo 3)

A native of the Deep South, William H. Johnson (1901-1970) studied painting at the National Academy of Design in New York City and at age 25 traveled to Europe and North Africa. He returned to New York in 1929 and won the prestigious Harmon Foundation gold medal in 1930.

After 1938, Johnson focused exclusively on African-American subjects and developed a deliberately primitive style, using limited palettes and painting on burlap and wood. Johnson became mentally ill in 1947 and was hospitalized in New York, where he died 23 years later.

Midsummer Night in Harlem,
Palmer Hayden,
1938
(color photo 4)

Palmer Hayden (1890-1973) was in Paris during most of the Harlem Renaissance, but the award-winning artist had lived in New York for several years before sailing for Europe. He knew and maintained contact with many of the black artists living and working in Harlem, and he exhibited in the annual Harmon Foundation shows from 1928 to 1932. Like Johnson, Hayden culti-vated a flat, consciously naive style during the late 1930s, and from that time on he concentrated almost exclusively on African-American themes. His greatest artistic exposure was in the 1967 exhibition "The Evolution of the African-American Artist," sponsored by the City University of New York, the Urban League, and the Harlem Cultural Council.

The Janitor Who Paints,
Palmer Hayden,
ca. 1937
(color photo 5)

James Weldon Johnson,
Laura Wheeler Waring,
ca. 1940s
(color photo 6)

Laura Wheeler Waring (1887-1948) studied art in Philadelphia and Paris. Her work is in the collections of several American art galleries, including the Smithsonian Institution, the National Archives, and the National Portrait Gallery, all in Washington, D.C. During the 1940s Waring and Betsy Graves Reyneau completed a series of 24 paintings for the Harmon Foundation, entitled *Portraits of Outstanding Americans of Negro Origin,* which includes portraits of a number of important figures of the Harlem Renaissance.

Portrait of Paul Bustill Robeson as Othello,
Betsy Graves Reyneau,
ca. 1940s
(color photo 7)

Aaron Douglas (1899-1979) was one of the first African-American artists to apply the qualities of primitive African sculpture to painting, using stylized figures, rhythmic lines, and narrative themes. Douglas's murals, portraits, and paintings—especially the series *Aspects of Negro Life*, which traces the cultural and social progress of African-Americans inspired other black artists to explore their heritage in their work.

Aspects of Negro Life: An Idyll of the Deep South,
Aaron Douglas,
1934
(color photo 8)

Aspects of Negro Life: The Negro in an African Setting,
Aaron Douglas,
1934
(color photo 9)

(continued from page 64)

sit around and represent the Negro race for them [because] she did it in such a racy fashion."

Hurston's life, though, wasn't all entertainment. She was born and raised in Eatonville, Florida, America's first all-black incorporated town, to a former sharecropper who became a three-term mayor of Eatonville. Hurston's mother died when she was about 13; neglected by her remarried father, Hurston began supporting herself at 14 with a variety of menial jobs. Her first short story appeared in Howard University's literary magazine. After arriving in Harlem, she became an associate editor for the avant-garde journal *Fire!!* and collaborated on several plays with writers such as Langston Hughes. She would eventually publish what is thought to be the first collection of African-American folklore compiled by a black American, *Mules and Men* (1935).

In March 1924, less than a year before Hurston's arrival in Harlem, *The Crisis* hosted a dinner party for about a dozen rising African-American literary stars in the Civic Club, the only upscale club in the city without race or gender restrictions. Originally, the event was intended to celebrate the recent publication of Jessie Fauset's *There Is Confusion*, but excitement had been building in the black literary community: in the three previous years, African-American authors such as W. E. B. Du Bois (*Darkwater*), Claude McKay (*Harlem Shadows*), and Jean Toomer (*Cane*) had produced works of considerable merit. Whites had also begun to take note, and although longstanding stereotypes had yet to be abolished from books and plays, black-themed productions were gaining in popularity.

The Crisis dinner was ultimately a literary symposium to which Fauset and her book became a postscript. Carl Van Doren, editor of the prestigious *Century* magazine; Charles Johnson; Locke; and Du Bois contributed their views on the significance of

A portrait of Zora Neale Hurston taken by her friend Carl Van Vechten. Probably the most colorful figure of the Harlem Renaissance, Hurston invited criticism from African Americans who felt that she used her flamboyance and storytelling talents to capitalize on white stereotypes about blacks.

this explosion of black culture. Declaring his faith in the "future of imaginative writing" among African Americans, Van Doren proclaimed, "What America decidedly needs at this moment is color, music, gusto, the free expression of gay or desperate moods. If the Negroes are not in a position to contribute these items, I do not know what Americans are."

By evening's end, Fauset had spoken only briefly, thanking the guests for their support. The dinner was perhaps typical of the way Fauset's work was acknowledged—although she has been lauded as one of the midwives of the Harlem Renaissance, her own work has often been overshadowed by her dedication to the movement.

Jessie Redmon Fauset was born in 1882 in Fredericksville, New Jersey, the seventh child of the

Reverend Redmond Fauset and Anna Fauset. Her mother died when she was very young, and her father remarried shortly after. Fauset graduated from the Philadelphia Girls' School in 1900 but was then denied admission to a local teacher's college; after she was put off by Bryn Mawr College, she attended Cornell University and in 1905 became the first black woman to graduate from the school.

One of the most literate of the Harlem Renaissance group, Fauset believed that the time of the "New Negro" had arrived. She urged other young black artists and writers in her circle to seize the opportunity to be recognized by the rest of America for the purpose of bettering race relations and establishing a black literary tradition. "We reasoned, 'Here is an audience waiting to hear the truth about us. Let us who are better qualified to present that truth than any white writer, try to do so,'" she said.

After the publication of her novel, Fauset took a leave of absence from *The Crisis* to travel in Europe and North Africa. Like many African-American writers and artists, Fauset found less racial discrimination abroad than in her native country. She wrote to her friend Arthur Spingarn that she had not felt so free since her teenage years. Despite the presence of a strong black community in Harlem, segregation laws still existed in the United States, and race relations had deteriorated after World War I. Fauset's observations of racial discrimination would appear in all four of her novels: *There Is Confusion* (1924), *Plum Bun* (1929), *The Chinaberry Tree* (1931), and *Comedy, American Style* (1933).

The novels of another Harlem author, Nella Larsen, also deal with skin color, privilege, racial heritage, and racial freedom—issues that figured largely in her own life. Nella Larsen was the daughter of an African-West Indian father and a Danish mother. Her father died when she was two; two years later her mother married a Danish man.

As the mouthpiece of the NAACP, The Crisis *offered African Americans a forum for their literature and social commentary.*

Larsen was raised in an all-white household and went to school in a predominantly white suburb of Chicago. In 1907 Larsen attended Fisk University Normal School, an all-black high school, for one year. There she met and married a physics professor named Elmer S. Imes. The marriage was brief. She would study at the University of Copenhagen in Denmark—her mother's homeland—before moving to New York to study nursing.

In 1922, after practicing nursing in Alabama and New York, Larsen became a children's librarian at the New York Public Library. Four years later, she began writing the first of two novels, *Quicksand*, which was published in 1928.

Like Langston Hughes, Nella Larsen sought relief from alienation and a place where she could feel like a member of a community. Like Jessie Fauset, she dealt with racial issues in her novels, in particular the mulatto's place in society—at the time a highly controversial topic. Although some critics cite fame and popularity as Larsen's guiding ambitions, the novel's treatment of middle-class black Americans was a significant and financially risky departure from most black American novels of that period. In reviewing her second novel, *Passing*, in the July 1929 edition of *The Crisis*, Du Bois wrote:

> If it did not treat a forbidden subject—the inter-marriage of a stodgy middle-class white man to a very beautiful and selfish octoroon—it would have an excellent chance to be hailed, selected and recommended. As it is, it will probably be given "the silence," with only the commendation of word of mouth.

In 1928 Larsen received a bronze medal from the prestigious Harmon Foundation, and in 1929 she received the first Guggenheim Fellowship ever given to a black woman. She would travel to Mallorca the following year to work on another novel, but it would never be published. Although she eventually returned to nursing, her literary themes of race, class, and the black person's place in society would be taken up by other African-American authors.

Another young artist who attended the Civic Club dinner in 1924 was Gwendolyn Bennett, a Texas native studying teaching at Columbia University. (It was Bennett and her librarian friend Regina Anderson, Ethel Ray Nance's roommate, who suggested the dinner to Charles Johnson.) Bennett would later transfer to the art program at Pratt Institute and accept a teaching position at Howard University in Washington, D.C.

Bennett found members of the black elite in Washington unsupportive, and following the path of Alain Locke, Jessie Fauset, Langston Hughes, and Aaron Douglas, she traveled to Paris on a scholarship. While studying at the École de Panthéon and the Sorbonne, she met a number of celebrated American expatriates including Gertrude Stein, Ernest Hemingway, and James Joyce. On one special occasion, she acted as a tour guide for singer and actor Paul Robeson, who had married Bennett's sorority sister and good friend Essie.

Bennett developed a talent for batik, an Indonesian fabric-printing process in which sections of cloth are coated in wax before the piece is dyed so that the wax design remains visible in the finished piece. Many of her works were displayed in Paris exhibitions, and she made an income by shipping some of her designs to New York for sale. She returned to her beloved Harlem in 1926, taking a position as assistant editor at *Opportunity*. There she authored a popular column called "Ebony Flute," which covered the social scene of Harlem.

Sculptor Augusta Savage also found creative refuge in Harlem. Born Augusta Fells in 1892 in Green Cove Springs, Florida, she was the seventh of 14 children of Cornelia and Edward Fells. Her

Though the works of Harlem Renaissance writers like Zora Neale Hurston and Langston Hughes remain well-known today, the novels of Jessie Fauset (above), one of the guiding forces of the Harlem Renaissance, are often overlooked.

father, a poor Methodist minister, strongly opposed his daughter's early interest in art. "My father licked me four or five times a week and almost whipped all the art out of me," she would later recall. Savage's sculpting talent was finally recognized in her senior year of high school when the school principal arranged to pay her one dollar a day for teaching clay modeling.

In 1907 Augusta married John T. Moore, and the following year she gave birth to her only child, Irene. Moore died several years later, and around 1915, Augusta married James Savage, a carpenter, whose name she would keep after their divorce in the early 1920s.

In September 1921 Savage left Irene in the care of her parents and traveled to New York City. She arrived with $4.60, took a job, and enrolled at the Cooper Union School of Art, where she completed the four-year program in three years.

Savage was 30 years old when she applied to a summer art program in Fountainebleau, near Paris, France. The exclusive school, which was sponsored by the French government, accepted only 100 American women each year, and although tuition was waived, Savage would need to raise money for airfare and living expenses. She arranged to receive funding from friends, but she was rejected by the school's admissions committee.

Savage suspected that she had been turned down because she was black, and she consulted Alfred W. Martin, the head of the Ethical Culture Society. Through him, she learned that the Fountainebleau committee felt that "southern" American students might not be comfortable with her presence and that they had therefore denied her admission in an effort to avoid embarrassment.

Enraged, Martin publicly exposed the committee—at that time a remarkable action by a white man on behalf of a black woman. Because those involved were prominent artists who had always taken pride in their "liberal" attitudes toward blacks, the situation quickly made news. Harlem's community leaders rallied around Savage, and in the May 20, 1923 issue of *New York World*, Savage herself spoke eloquently about the issue:

> I don't care much for myself because I will get along all right here, but other and better colored students might wish to apply [to Fountainebleau] sometime. . . . Democracy is a strange thing. My brother was good enough to be accepted into one of the regiments that saw service in France during the war, but it seems his sister is not good enough to be a guest of the country for which he fought. . . . How am I to compete with other American artists if I am not to be given the same opportunity?

The controversy grew. Emmett J. Scott of Howard University labeled Savage's exclusion from the program the artistic equivalent to a lynching. When the Fountainebleau committee refused to speak with the press, Alfred Martin sailed to France to appeal to its members in person.

None of these efforts, however, gained Savage's admission into the school. What she did gain was the allegiance of Hermon A. MacNeil, a sculptor known for his sensitive portrayals of African Americans—and a committee member who did not agree with the committee's decision about Savage. As a young artist, MacNeil had shared a Paris studio with Henry Ossawa Tanner, the first black painter to receive international recognition, and he vividly recalled Tanner's stories about racism in America.

Unable to sway the other Fountainebleau committee members, MacNeil invited Savage to become his personal student, and in time he became one of her most important mentors. However, while she earned fame as a fighter for black civil rights, Savage was also branded as a "troublemaker" in the close-knit, influential community of curators, crit-

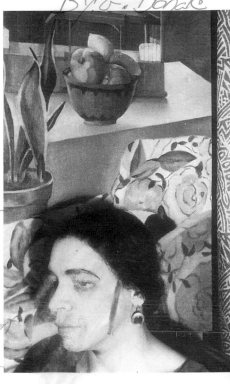

Nella Larsen in 1932, photographed by Carl Van Vechten. Larsen often incorporated her feelings of alienation into her novels, which focus on the lives of middle-class blacks and those of mixed heritage.

Gamin, *Augusta Savage's award-winning sculpture, belies the artist's assertion that she had "created nothing really beautiful, really lasting." One of Savage's primary aims was to inspire future generations to create art: "[I]f I can inspire one of these youngsters to develop the talent I know they possess," she said of her students, "then my monument will be in their work."*

ics, foundation personnel, art dealers, and other artists, and her professional life suffered as a result.

Fountainebleau was one of a number of struggles for Augusta Savage. Widowed and divorced by age 31, she bore sole financial responsibility for her large family. After her father suffered a paralyzing stroke, she brought her parents from Florida to live with her. Not long after, the family home was destroyed in a hurricane, which also killed one of her brothers. Savage brought the rest of her family—eight people in all—into her three-room apartment on West 137th Street in Harlem and took work in the steam laundries of Manhattan.

While working, Savage would encourage herself by thinking of Meta Vaux Warrick Fuller, a black sculptress who in 1899 managed to secure a place in Rome's Colarossi Academy and became a student of the famed sculptor Auguste Rodin. Fuller's success inspired Savage to continue her creative work, and she spent nearly all of her free time in the Harlem branch of the New York Public Library studying artists and art history.

Her labors did not go unnoticed. Sadie Peterson, one of the librarians who worked where Savage studied, was impressed by her perseverance. Peterson arranged for the Friends of the Library to commission from Savage a bust of W. E. B. Du Bois. The finished piece, presented to the library in 1923, earned critical acclaim and additional commissions for its creator—among them a bust of the black nationalist Marcus Garvey.

Savage was one of the first artists to deal consistently with black physiognomy, or physical features. One of her best-known works is the award-winning *Gamin*, an informal portrait reputedly modeled after her nephew, Ellis Ford, who lived in Harlem. Although the sculpture represents a specific individual, it also conveys the rebelliousness, discomfort, energy, and willfullness of thousands of urban youths just entering their teens. For *Gamin*, she was awarded a Julius Rosenwald Fellowship to study in Paris in 1929. In 1931 she won a second Rosenwald fellowship, allowing her to remain in Paris for another year, and a Carnegie Foundation grant to travel to France, Belgium, and Germany.

After returning to Harlem, Savage founded her own school, the Savage Studio of Arts and Crafts, and in 1934 she became the first African-American member of the National Association of Women Painters and Sculptors. Three years later, she was appointed the first director of the Harlem Community Art Center.

Savage eventually was forced to end her career for lack of funding. However, like fellow artist Gwendolyn Bennett and literary colleagues Zora Neale Hurston, Jessie Fauset, and Nella Larsen, she had succeeded in breaking many of the barriers facing black women in the arts and had made vital contributions to the African-American cultural explosion known as the Harlem Renaissance.

6

Patrons of the Renaissance

MORE THAN ANY OTHER white American, Carl Van Vechten became synonymous with the Harlem Renaissance. He was introduced to Harlem in 1924, when he and his wife, Russian-born actress Fania Marinoff, accompanied Walter and Gladys White to an NAACP dance at Happy Rhone's Black and White Club. Van Vechten's fascination with black culture grew to such a degree that *Time* magazine acidly commented that he had "been playing with Negroes lately." Mexican artist Miguel Covarrubias was even more direct. Under the title, "A Prediction," he drew a portrait of Carl Van Vechten with black skin.

Van Vechten first achieved recognition as a music critic for the *New York Times*, and it was Harlem's music that drew him to the neighborhood. But even Van Vechten did not believe that his fas-

Vibraphonist Lionel Hampton (left), clarinetist Benny Goodman (center), and drummer Gene Krupa (right) perform before a black audience in Harlem. Goodman was one of the first to break the color barrier among American musicians by hiring blacks for his band.

cination with Harlem would last. "Jazz, the blues, Negro spirituals, all stimulate me enormously for the moment," said a sardonic Van Vechten to newspaperman and critic H. L. Mencken in 1924. "Doubtless, I shall discard them too in time."

Van Vechten was wrong, however—his interest in Harlem would be lasting. Writing and contributing amateur photography for such publications as *Vanity Fair*, he would become one of the most important and influential chroniclers of Harlem's literary and musical talent—and so well-known that the popular song "Go Harlem" contained the lyric, "Go inspectin' like Van Vechten."

Van Vechten was one of a number of white Americans whose interest in Harlem was sparked by its glamorous and exotic reputation. After the *Opportunity* awards dinner in May 1925, the *Herald Tribune* remarked on the African "love of color, warmth, rhythm, and the whole sensuous life," stating that "one of fate's quaint but by no means impossible revenges" would be that "the Negro's real contribution to American life should be in the field of art." That year, Harlem's growing fame as the heart of an African-American cultural renaissance would draw scores of sophisticated whites into the neighborhood.

Many blacks were also pleasantly surprised to find themselves "in vogue." As the black novelist and physician Rudolph Fisher remarked in 1927, "Negro stock is going up and everybody's buying." Charles Johnson, though, would not have been among them. With his colleagues, such as James Weldon Johnson and Alain Locke, he was responsible for orchestrating the advent of the "New Negro." Johnson strongly believed that the only way to raise the status of African Americans in a racist society was through the intellect. By 1925, he had turned the National Urban League's prestigious magazine, *Opportunity*, into a major voice in the

Carl Van Vechten, shown here with his wife, Fania Marinoff, in Venice in 1914 (left), and an advertisement for Nigger Heaven *illustrated by Aaron Douglas (above). Though some prominent authors praised the accuracy of Van Vechten's portrayal of black Harlem, many others were outraged by what they believed was a white stereotyped view of African Americans.*

Harlem Renaissance.

The term "New Negro" first emerged after World War I, when black leaders called on their followers to demand their civil rights. One black publication stated in 1920:

> The New Negro realizes that there cannot be any qualified equality. . . . [The New Negro] is the product of the same world-wide forces that have brought into being the great liberal and radical movements that are now seizing the reins of political, economic and social power in all of the civilized countries of the world.

By the mid-1920s, the term had come to refer to members of Harlem's burgeoning literary movement. "The New Negro writers," observed historian

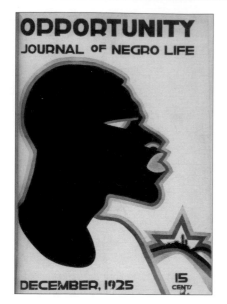

Like Du Bois and many of his colleagues, Charles Johnson strongly believed that black equality could only be achieved through the intellect. By 1925, Johnson had shaped the National Urban League's prestigious Opportunity *magazine into a major voice of the Harlem Renaissance.*

Jervis Anderson in his 1981 book *This Was Harlem: 1900-1950*, "could be said to represent in art what the race militants had represented in politics—not an appeal to compassion and social redress but a bold assertion of self."

Some of the new literary stars to whom the term was applied accepted the classification with humor. Zora Neale Hurston poked fun at the solemn reformers of the NAACP, calling them "Negrotarians"; even more outrageous to some observers was her cheerfully irreverent term for the group of young black literati to which she herself belonged: she called them the "Niggerati." In his novel *Infants of the Spring*, Wallace Thurman returned the barb by thinly disguising his friend Hurston as a character who proclaims, "Being a Negro writer these days is a racket and I'm going to make the most out of it while it lasts. . . . About twice a year I manage to sell a story. It is acclaimed. I am a genius in the making. Thank God for this Negro literary renaissance! Long may it flourish!"

The Harlem Renaissance was much more than simply a white fad, but the extent of white interest and support—and the necessity of responding to it—shaped the movement in many ways. Having cultivated his new fascination with Harlem, Carlo, as Van Vechten's friends called him, became a kind of human Statue of Liberty for the neighborhood, ushering curious whites and downtowners into the area. Legend has it that he guided a very drunk William Faulkner from one Harlem club to another until sunrise, with Faulkner requesting the tune "St. Louis Blues" of each club band.

Van Vechten also invited Harlemites to the West Side, where he lived with his wife Fania in an apartment on West 55th Street. Van Vechten's spectacular parties were filled with both black and white notables: George Gershwin, Tallulah Bankhead, and Theodore Dreiser mixed with Paul Robeson, James

Weldon Johnson, and Ethel Waters. In his book *Blues: An Anthology*, composer and conductor W. C. Handy, a frequent visitor to the Van Vechten home, would credit his host for being "the pen that set tongues to wagging, ears listening and feet dancing to the blues."

Gradually, Van Vechten became more of a Harlem insider than many of its working-class residents, who were removed from the glitter and acclaim of the black elite. He cultivated a friendship with James Weldon Johnson; he introduced Paul Robeson to Lawrence Brown, who would become Robeson's arranger and accompanist, and arranged Robeson's first concert at Town Hall. He showed Paris to Ethel Waters and became a mentor to Langston Hughes, Nella Larsen, and Rudolph Fisher.

Van Vechten had encountered very few blacks during his childhood: only two lived in Cedar Rapids, Iowa, where he grew up. Although his father, one of the founders of Piney Woods, the first school for blacks in Mississippi, taught his son to respect blacks, Van Vechten often acted decidedly superior in his dealings with black Harlemites. Author Arnold Rampersand has noted that although Van Vechten was a patron of the Harlem Renaissance, the opinions of the movement's principal figures were mixed. While Langston Hughes found the Van Vechten gatherings a heady thrill, Claude McKay referred to Van Vechten as "a white man who bothered to be subtle in his patronizing."

After striking up a conversation with a young Langston Hughes at the *Opportunity* dinner in 1925, Van Vechten extended an invitation for Hughes to visit him at his home and urged him to bring along some of his work. Less than two weeks later, Van Vechten had placed Hughes's manuscript with Knopf and had suggested a title: *The Weary Blues*. The young poet was astonished at Van Vechten's power and generosity. "How quickly it's all been done!" he exclaimed. "How shall I thank you? As the old folks say, I'll have to walk sideways to keep from flying!"

Hughes's success accorded him even more acclaim in Harlem's literary circles. "Undoubtedly, the greatest kind of future is stretching before you," wrote Jessie Fauset, the first to publish Hughes (in *The Brownies' Book*). A proud Hughes sent copies of his publicity photo to his "Auntie" Mary Reed in Kansas, a family friend who had helped to raise Hughes after his grandmother's death.

Although Hughes was anxious to finish college, Van Vechten thought it would be a waste of time and persuaded him to write his autobiography instead. Hughes was not eager to turn his attention to painful childhood memories of abandonment and poverty. "I hate to think backwards," he told Van Vechten. "It isn't amusing . . . I am still too much enmeshed in the affects of my young life to write clearly about it." But Van Vechten was insistent and even refused to help Hughes obtain a college scholarship. There was no money in education, he said.

Hughes nevertheless found the courage to defy his mentor. The following year he enrolled in Lincoln University, a predominantly black college in rural Pennsylvania. Both Countee Cullen and Jessie Fauset had tried to get Hughes into an Ivy League university, telling him that he would miss out on the important relationships he needed to establish to be successful. However, Hughes felt that direct contact with people like him was essential for the kind of writing he wanted to do. "You see, I'm going into seclusion," he wrote Van Vechten just before leaving for Lincoln. Professing to be "weary of the world," he declared, "I hope nobody there reads poetry."

Hughes thrived at Lincoln and felt more at home there than he had anywhere else in his life.

As a "blues poet," he performed throughout the country with the university's vocal quartet. He published his epic essay, "The Negro Artist and the Racial Mountain" in *The Nation*, and his impressive attempt at modernism, "A House in Taos," won first prize in the prestigious Poetry Society of America's undergraduate poetry contest.

Hughes's second collection of poems, *Fine Clothes to the Jew*, was published in February 1927. Unlike his first book, however, Hughes's sophomore effort was both a financial and critical disappointment. He was criticized for the seemingly anti-Semitic nature of the title. Several of the characters are drunks and prostitutes, and sex and violence are among the themes incorporated into the poems. The black newspaper the Amsterdam News called the author a "Sewer Dweller," and the Philadelphia Tribune thought it regrettable that Hughes had pilfered his talent with his "obsession for the more degenerate elements" of society. Hughes, however, wrote about the darker side of life not only because it attracted him but also because few others had written about it. "My poems are indelicate," he admitted. "But so is life."

In mid-April 1927, a few months after the publication of *Fine Clothes to the Jew*, Hughes met a white woman in her seventies who in time would have an important, almost crushing effect on his life. Her name was Charlotte Osgood Mason, and she was introduced to him through Alain Locke. The widow of a well-known psychologist and physician, Mason was an heiress to generations of wealth. Her Park Avenue apartment, which afforded a dramatic view of Manhattan, was filled with exquisite collections of European, African, and American Indian art.

Having been told by Locke that Hughes was an up-and-coming poet, Mason summoned Hughes to her apartment to tell him about her hope of foster-

Langston Hughes, photo—graphed by Carl Van Vechten, one of Hughes's first mentors.

ing black art and writing. She believed that blacks, like Native Americans, were "primitive people" who were in closer contact with nature and their natural impulses than were whites. Insisting that she meant this not as an insult but as praise, she told him that her mission was to save the world—at least to save those things that were natural and spontaneous in the world—by making the art and writing of blacks better known. She told Hughes:

> As the fire burned in me, I had the mystical vision of a great bridge reaching from Harlem to the heart of Africa, across which the Negro world, that our white United States had done everything to annihilate, should see the flaming pathway . . . and recover the treasures their people had had in the beginning of African life on earth.

Langston Hughes was taken aback not only by her wealth but by her warm reception. "I found her instantly one of the most delightful women I had ever met, witty and charming, kind and sympathetic." Mason wanted Hughes (as well as Locke and Hurston) to help her realize her vision. She would give him money to support his work, and he would acknowledge her guidance in the direction his work would take. For Hughes, who had been poor all his life, her offer was one he could not afford to turn down.

Calling Hughes her "winged poet Child" and "a noble silent Indian Chief," she insisted that he call her "Godmother." In addition to his needing financial help, something in Hughes's emotional makeup responded deeply to Mason, and he agreed. He maintained, "No one else had ever been so thoughtful of me, or so interested in the things I wanted to do, or so kind and generous toward me."

That summer, Hughes traveled to the South. He read some of his poems at Fisk University in Nashville, Tennessee, then continued farther south to Memphis, Tennessee, and New Orleans,

Louisiana. This poetry-reading tour was the first of many. It was also his first trip to the South. He viewed the trip as an opportunity not only to make money with his readings but also to get to know southern blacks better.

Zora Neale Hurston, a southerner who had written to Hughes about the wealth of black folklore in the South, was at the time on an anthropological field trip from Barnard. In Mobile, Alabama, Hughes met Hurston and the two drove back to New York City together. After they arrived, Hughes immediately introduced Hurston to Mason. Impressed with the young woman's knowledge and her southern background, Mason presented her with an offer similar to the one she had given Hughes. "I must tell the tales, sing the songs, do the dances and repeat the raucous sayings and doings of the Negro farthest down," Hurston later reported. As with Hughes, though, the stipend she received suited her purposes, and Hurston and Mason became friends. "My relations with Godmother were curious," she would later recall. "Laugh if you will, but there was and is a psychic bond between us."

Four years later, however, Hurston would be dismissed by Mason. The previous year, Mason had treated Hughes in the same manner, declaring blacks "a lost cause." Hughes was emotionally—and financially—devastated. Although he had often chafed at Mason's arbitrary and rigid rules, he had also felt loved and protected by her. Without her support, he felt rudderless and adrift.

Despite Hughes's numerous attempts to regain Mason's friendship, she refused to see him. "I do not wish to lose you," he wrote, declaring that the money he had received from her was unimportant. "I would still love you as deeply as ever because you are to me more beautiful than anybody else in the world." Years later, Hughes would write of his painful last meeting with Mason in her apartment:

Writers Langston Hughes and Zora Neale Hurston and painter Aaron Douglas all benefited from the patronage of Charlotte Osgood Mason. But Mason's demands for strict control over their subject matter and her unwavering belief in blacks as "primitive people" eventually alienated all three artists.

Walter White (left) served as chief assistant to James Weldon Johnson (right) during Johnson's term as the executive secretary of the NAACP. Both men reviewed Van Vechten's Nigger Heaven *favorably. Johnson called the author "one of the most vital forces in bringing about the artistic emergence of the Negro in America."*

[W]hen I think about it, even now something happens in the pit of my stomach that makes me ill. That beautiful room, that had been so full of light and help and understanding for me, suddenly became like a trap closing in, faster and faster, the room darker and darker, until the light went out with a sudden crash.

In December 1925, while Hughes was preparing to attend Lincoln University, Carl Van Vechten finished the second draft of *Nigger Heaven*, a new novel he had been writing. He asked James Weldon Johnson and Walter White to review it. He also asked his father to read it. "I have, myself, never spoken of a colored man as a 'nigger,'" the appalled elder Van Vechten wrote to his son. He urged him to change the title. "It would not be understood," he wrote. "I feel certain you should change it."

Van Vechten's title came from a phrase describing the segregated balcony seats in theaters. He had used it as a metaphor for the way Harlem was situated over lower Manhattan:

> We sit in our places in the gallery of this New York theatre and watch the white world sitting down below in the good seats in the orchestra. Occasionally they turn their faces up towards us, their hard, cruel faces, to laugh or sneer, but they never beckon. It doesn't seem to occur to them that Nigger Heaven is crowded, that there isn't another seat, that something has to be done.

Nearly every character in *Nigger Heaven* was modeled after a prominent Harlem figure: the prim and proper Mary Love is widely assumed to have been based on Jessie Fauset, black millionairess Adora Boniface is a fictional A'Lelia Walker, and the sophisticated and cultured Underwoods are Grace and James Weldon Johnson. Even the character of Gareth Johns, a white novelist, is believed to be Van Vechten himself.

Nigger Heaven was an instant and controversial bestseller. The salacious title intrigued whites who were eager to hear fantastic tales of Harlem life. As with Hughes's second book of poems, much of the criticism focused on its title. "Anyone who would call a book *Nigger Heaven* would call a Negro Nigger," fumed the black publication the *New York News*. W. E. B. Du Bois considered the novel nothing short of a personal affront:

> [Nigger heaven] means, in common parlance, a nasty sordid corner into which black folks are herded, and yet a place in which they in crass ignorance are fools enough to enjoy. Harlem is no such place as that, and no one knows this better than Carl Van Vechten.

Alain Locke and Countee Cullen agreed with Du Bois in his criticism—for the next 14 years, Cullen would refuse even to speak to Van Vechten. Still, Langston Hughes, Nella Larsen, Wallace Thurman, and Charles Johnson supported Van Vechten. "You managed to get what many Negroes will regard as 'family secrets,'" Johnson wrote to Van Vechten. "The long, eloquent discussions of 'passing,' residential segregation, special indignities visited upon well-bred Afro-Americans . . . envy of poor blacks and self-hatred of their betters—all this Van Vechten recorded with striking fidelity," wrote David Levering Lewis in *When Harlem Was in Vogue*.

White supporters, meanwhile, also spoke out. Gertrude Stein praised the novel as "rather perfectly done," and F. Scott Fitzgerald and Mabel Dodge applauded Van Vechten for his realism. The author's brother Ralph applauded his efforts, joking that he "had done more for the Negro than anyone since Abraham Lincoln." Playwright Avery Hopwood pushed the line even further. Many whites with whom he spoke were surprised, he said, "to hear about your negro strain, but I tell them that your best friends already knew." Van Vechten's estimation of himself as a cultural broker escalated as *Nigger Heaven* continued to sell. He announced that his next books would "take up the Chinese and the Jews."

When Claude McKay published *Home to Harlem* in 1928, *Tattler Magazine* derided the author for having "outniggered Mr. Van Vechten." *Home to Harlem*, though, became the first novel by a writer of the Harlem Renaissance to become a bestseller. In the *New York Times*, reviewer John Chamberlain proclaimed it a "book that is beaten through with the rhythm of life that is the jazz rhythm . . . the real thing in rightness." Charlotte Mason, who deplored Van Vechten's novel, praised *Home to Harlem* as a novel in which "life and laughter is ready to burst into such brilliant sunshine."

Claude McKay's 1928 novel, Home to Harlem, *received similar criticism to that of Van Vechten's* Nigger Heaven. *But because McKay (left) was himself black, many condemned his work as racially disloyal.*

The critical outrage that met *Home to Harlem's* release was different than that expressed upon the publication of Van Vechten's book. It was one thing for an white author to scandalize Harlem with salacious tales; it was quite another for a black person, who had spoken so eloquently of his race in his poems, to portray Harlem as a breeding ground of wickedness.

McKay never had been comfortable or patient with Harlem's black elite, however. While Van Vechten's novel describes a Harlem of young black millionaires throwing parties in their country mansions and hostesses conducting literary discussions in French, McKay's book focuses on the poor, the debauched, and the criminals of black urban life. "I consider [my book] a really proletarian novel," he declared, "but I don't expect the nice radicals to see that it is."

In many ways, Van Vechten and McKay both struggled with the theme of primitivism in black and black-related culture. While many white patrons of black American art and literature extolled its "primitive" nature, blacks thought the term demeaning and synonymous with "uneducated" or "uncivilized."

In the 1920s Africa itself was still referred to as the Dark Continent, a wild, unsophisticated, and primitive place. What white patrons seemed to want from black artists was for them to remain unsophisticated and uneducated. Van Vechten, for example, discouraged Hughes from seeking an advanced degree, fearing it would taint his work. Mason would reject Hughes's poems as "not you" when she thought they reflected a sophistication that contradicted her notions of black art. Hughes would later write that Mason wanted him "to be primitive and know and feel the intuitions of the primitive." Yet, he continued,

> [U]nfortunately, I did not feel the primitive surging within me, and so I could not live and write as though I did. I was only an American Negro—who had loved the surface of Africa and the rhythms of Africa—but I was not Africa. I was Chicago and Kansas City and Broadway and Harlem.

Du Bois and other elder statesmen of the Harlem Renaissance criticized authors like Hughes and McKay, who wrote about gamblers and numbers runners, and they took painter Archibald Motley to task for portraying a nightclub scene in his painting *Bronzeville*. They believed that it was essential to present the black community to the rest of the world in the best possible light.

At the same time, Du Bois also realized that the time had come for African Americans to declare their independence from the world of white arts and literature. "It is not that we are ashamed of our color and blood," Du Bois declared in 1920. "We are instinctively and almost unconsciously ashamed of the caricatures done of our darker shades. . . . Off with these thought chains and inchoate soul-shrinkings, and let us train ourselves to see beauty in 'black.'"

As many artists of the Harlem Renaissance discovered, however, the thought chains of America— both white and black—were strong. Writing, painting, or sculpting for the approval of critics, patrons, or even peers would not bring freedom or fulfillment. Regardless of skin color, the only true obligation of an artist was, as Countee Cullen put it, to "find his treasure where his heart lies."

7

Free Within Ourselves

FIRE . . . flaming, burning, searing, and penetrating
far beneath the superficial items of
the flesh to boil the sluggish blood. . . .
FIRE . . . weaving vivid, hot designs upon an ebon
bordered loom and satisfying pagan
thirst for beauty unadorned . . . and
flesh is sweet and real . . . the soul
an inward flush of fire . . . Beauty
. . . flesh on fire—on fire in the
furnace of life blazing. . . .
"Fy-ah,
Fy-ah, Lawd,
Fy-ah gonna burn ma soul!"

—Langston Hughes and Wallace Thurman
from the foreword to *Fire!!* Magazine

An Aaron Douglas illustration from James Weldon Johnson's poetry collection God's Trombones, 1927.

FOR THE GROUP of young writers Hurston had named the Niggerati, the differences between Alain Locke's view of black art and literature as a weapon against racism and Du Bois's belief that art must be politically useful were unimportant. Whether or not their work had any propaganda value was immaterial to these writers.

Nor did they embrace the cultural conservatism of writers like James Weldon Johnson. Hurston and her allies believed that, while men like Johnson paid lip service to the richness of black heritage, they balked at publishing anything that seemed *too* rich, worried about reinforcing white stereotypes—and about frightening away white financial support.

The Niggerati were determined to create art rooted in the life actually lived by ordinary black people.

Out of this determination they created the literary magazine *Fire!!*, which debuted in November 1926. Named after a poem by Langston Hughes and Wallace Thurman, *Fire!!* was intended to shock the sensibilities of the Renaissance midwives. It succeeded: its finely crafted stories on such "forbidden" subjects as child prostitution and homosexuality horrified the very establishment on which its success depended.

The magazine was born one evening in 1926, when Zora Neale Hurston, Langston Hughes, Wallace Thurman, and Richard Bruce Nugent met at the apartment of artist Aaron Douglas. For Thurman, who was chief editor, the magazine became a consuming passion. While working as circulation manager of the white-owned publication *World Tomorrow*, Thurman went into debt to finance the first issue of *Fire!!*. The new magazine meant everything to him. An open homosexual and an alcoholic, Thurman had long felt as though he was on the periphery of the Harlem Renaissance and of society itself. *Fire!!* offered him a chance to prove himself.

A native of Utah, Thurman grew up in Los Angeles, California. He tried with middling success to launch a West Coast version of the Harlem Renaissance with his magazine *The Outlet* before moving east to the center of the movement. He arrived in Harlem in 1925, eager to catch up with those already in the midst of the resurgence. "We're all in the same bunch with Langston Hughes and Countee Cullen and all the rest," he explained to one reviewer. "But they've arrived and the rest of us are on the make."

Regardless of the artistic freedom Harlem afforded in the 1920s, skin color still denoted privilege, even among blacks. A light-skinned black,

Believing that black art and literature must be founded on the lives of real African Americans, Wallace Thurman (left) nearly bankrupted himself to produce Fire!! magazine. Its single issue, with cover image by Aaron Douglas, is shown above.

like Langston Hughes, Nella Larsen, or Jessie Fauset, would be more readily accepted by the black elite. Consequently, Thurman, who was very dark-skinned, could not gain admission to this select group. The fair-skinned Richard Bruce Nugent remarked upon first meeting Thurman before a dinner, "There was this little black boy with a sneering nose . . . I couldn't eat . . . How dare he be so black?" Although Thurman and Nugent eventually became friends, Thurman never forgot Nugent's initial snub. He would treat such intraracial prejudice in his novel, *The Darker the Berry*, fully intending to shock his readers in the way that Van Vechten and McKay had done.

Thurman's contribution to *Fire!!* was a story called "Cordelia the Crude," in which the male protagonist's compassion for a child prostitute prevents

One of the finest artists to emerge from the Harlem Renaissance, Archibald Motley, shown here in 1932 with one of his paintings, believed that African Americans deserved "to be represented in [their] true perspective, with dignity, honesty, integrity, intelligence, and understanding."

her from finding another profession. Richard B. Nugent's "Smoke, Lilies and Jade" features Beauty, an allegorical figure who changes into the protagonist's fiancée, and depicts opium-induced fantasies and homosexuality.

Du Bois and Locke, among others, treated the magazine with patronizing disdain, overlooking the superiority of its content as compared to the writing that had appeared in *The New Negro*. "I have just tossed the first issue of *Fire!!* into the fire," a reviewer for the Baltimore *Afro-American* sneered. Countee Cullen received a letter from a friend telling him that the mere mention of the publication evoked such hurt feelings in Du Bois that "he would hardly talk" to him.

Yet the magazine's only issue was a masterpiece of the Harlem Renaissance. Hurston's *Color Struck* appeared in the issue, as well as the short story "Sweat," considered the finest piece of fiction that

Hurston wrote during her association with the Harlem Renaissance. The poems of Hughes, Cullen, Arna Bontemps, and Helene Johnson were also published. Aaron Douglas, who became one of the most important visual artists of the movement, contributed several drawings. (Hughes would later say of *Fire!!* that it had to be printed "on good paper . . . worthy of the drawings of Aaron Douglas.")

Douglas was the son of a domestic worker. As a child growing up in Kansas, he saw a magazine illustrated by one of the premier black painters of turn-of-the-century America, Henry Ossawa Tanner. "It was his painting of Christ and Nicodemus meeting in the moonlight on a rooftop," Douglas recalled. "I spent hours poring over it and that helped to lead me to deciding to become an artist."

Douglas arrived in New York with more formal training than most of the other aspiring artists streaming into Harlem. He had earned a degree in drawing, painting, and art history from the University of Nebraska, where he was the only black student. Such isolation never seemed to bother the even-tempered Douglas. "Sturdy and friendly," as he later described himself, he was popular with students and faculty. After receiving a degree in fine arts from the University of Kansas, he taught art for two years. Like many young American artists in the 1920s, he dreamed of studying in Paris, but friends persuaded him to go to New York instead. He arrived in 1925—at the height of the Harlem Renaissance.

With an introduction from Charles S. Johnson, Douglas met Winold Reiss, the son of a Bavarian landscapist, who had established himself as a gifted artist especially skillful with detailed work. Meeting Reiss at his studio, the 27-year-old Douglas felt a sense of awe. Except during a class tour as a student, he'd never been in a professional artist's studio before.

Like many Europeans who emigrated to the United States, Reiss was fascinated by the decorative and cultural art of Native Americans. The bold style of his Native American-influenced colored drawings led Johnson and Locke to recruit him to design and illustrate the "Harlem" issue of *Survey Graphic*. Reiss became a prominent mentor of minority students and took on Douglas at no charge.

Under Reiss, Douglas began cultivating his own style. Adopting some of the techniques of the Cubists, he distilled objects into their most basic shapes and used flat, elongated silhouettes of black figures with startling effectiveness. His paintings are masterpieces of color, featuring Egyptian design elements that symbolize black Americans' mysterious African past, and concentric rings that represent the importance of education in forging an African-American future. When Alain Locke published *Survey Graphic* in book form as *The New Negro*, he devoted six pages to Douglas's work. The artist's black-and-white drawings were also featured in *Vanity Fair*, and some of his most outstanding pieces appeared in James Weldon Johnson's book of poems, *God's Trombones*, published in 1925.

While working on a mural for Club Ebony, a popular Harlem night spot, Douglas was introduced to Charlotte Mason, who immediately purchased two of his paintings. Douglas received $250 in all, more money than he had ever received for his work, and joined the Godmother's payroll with Hurston and Hughes.

From the start, Douglas chafed at his patron's demands. She called him constantly with suggestions and advice, and when he accepted a scholarship at the Merion Art School in Pennsylvania, she demanded that he return at once to New York and was furious when he refused. As with Hughes and Hurston, Mason feared that an advanced education would ruin Douglas's "primitive" instincts.

Less than a year later, Douglas severed his financial ties to Mason. He married Alta Mae Sawyer, and the two saved enough money to travel abroad. They eventually settled in Paris. Like sculptor Augusta Savage and painters William H. Johnson, Archibald Motley, and Palmer Hayden, Douglas's art would reflect the full beauty, joy, and humanity of black Americans. In 1929, Motley seemed to speak for all the black artists of the Harlem Renaissance when he said:

> For many years, artists have depicted the Negro as the ignorant, southern "darky" to be portrayed on canvas as something humorous; an old southern black Negro gulping a large piece of watermelon; one with a banjo on his knee, possibly a "crapshooter" or a cotton-picker or a chicken thief. This material is obsolete and I sincerely hope that with the progress the Negro has made, he deserves to be represented in his true perspective, with dignity, honesty, integrity, intelligence and understanding . . . In my painting, I have tried to paint the Negro as I have seen him and as I feel him, in myself without adding or detracting, just being frankly honest.

One manner of raising the portrayal of blacks above stereotypes was to represent them exactly as they were. No medium could accomplish this with as much power and immediacy as photography—and no one in Harlem in the 1920s had mastered the art of photography like James Van Der Zee.

Van Der Zee was born in Lenox, Massachusetts, not far from Du Bois's childhood home of Great Barrington. At 12 he won his first camera for selling perfume packets. Van Der Zee remained passionate about photography, but he was a musician by profession, a violinist who formed the Harlem Orchestra shortly after arriving in New York.

Van Der Zee found it difficult to make a steady living performing, however, and in 1917 he resolved to turn his lifelong hobby into a profitable business.

Future Expectations (Wedding Day), *1926, one of James Van Der Zee's most remarkable photographs.*

His first portrait studio, Guaranty Photo, opened on 135th Street in the heart of Harlem. He quickly became the most sought-after photographer in the thriving black community, where people were anxious to preserve on film the infectious good feelings and fond memories of the time.

Van Der Zee had a gift for posing his clients in becoming and often unusual settings. In one typical photograph, which he called *Future Expectations (Wedding Day)*, a beautiful young Harlem bride poses before a painted backdrop of a fireplace next to a handsome young man dressed in a tuxedo. Sitting on the floor beside the couple is a shadowy figure of a young girl holding a doll—suggesting the newlyweds' future family.

Van Der Zee photographed the elite of Harlem, from writers and blues singers to boxing champion Jack Johnson and religious leader Adam Clayton Powell Sr. But one did not have to be wealthy or socially prominent to be one of his subjects. He also photographed men in billiard rooms, children playing in the street, and friends and relatives attending neighborhood funerals and weddings. To Van Der Zee's observant eye, everyone and everything in Harlem merited attention. When asked to explain his popularity as Harlem's most renowned photographer, Van Der Zee replied, "Well, it seems as though I had a personal interest in the pictures . . . sometimes they seemed to be more valuable to me than they did to the people I was photographing because I put my heart and soul into them."

Van Der Zee's statement illuminates not only his own work, but that of other artists and intellectuals of the period, all of whom were dedicated to expressing the spirit, the hard work, the joys, and the sorrows of thousands of black Americans living in a society that largely rejected their contributions. Political assertiveness, racial pride, and a growing respect for African culture fueled the renaissance. But as the 1920s came to a close, economic forces beyond the control of individual Harlemites brought the age of the "New Negro" to a crashing halt and shattered the lives of millions of Americans.

8

The Last Leaf on the Tree

THE CRASH OF THE New York Stock Exchange on October 29, 1929 ravaged the entire nation, marking the beginning of an economic depression that lasted well into World War II. Millions of unskilled laborers lost their jobs, and skilled laborers who managed to keep working suffered a drastic drop in income. Soup kitchens were set up to offer free meals to the unemployed, and the government established federal relief funds to be distributed to the needy across the country. During the Great Depression, as this period came to be known, between one-quarter and one-third of the country's work force was unemployed.

African Americans suffered even more severely during this period: black unemployment soared to about 50 percent nationwide, and in some large cities it reached even higher rates—65 percent in Atlanta, Georgia, and 80 percent in Norfolk, Virginia. African-American workers were usually the first to be let go; nearly half of those who lost their jobs had been domestic servants and were replaced by white workers, many of whom had previously considered such work too menial.

Puzzled and worried, depositors mill around the locked and guarded doors of a bank in 1932. More than 10,000 banks failed during the Great Depression, wiping out the life savings of millions of Americans.

All over the country, lines of needy people formed outside local Department of Welfare buildings seeking federal relief money. Even when working, African Americans on the whole earned less than white workers. During the Depression, local relief efforts often did not reach as many blacks as whites, and in the South, unemployed blacks received only 60 percent of what unemployed whites received each month.

Unemployment was not the only burden to fall disproportionately on the black community. During

*Adam Clayton Powell Sr.
(center left) poses with members of the Abyssinian Baptist
Church outside the building.
During the Depression, black
churches were more than spiritual havens, providing money,
clothing, housing, and other
necessities to those in distress.*

the 1930s, African Americans experienced higher rates of illness, infant death, malnutrition, and suicide than whites. Even more ominously, lynchings increased as whites attacked blacks whom they regarded as competitors for employment.

In Harlem, the Great Depression was devastating. According to a 1930 *New York Herald Tribune* report, the 1929 stock market crash had "produced five times as much unemployment in Harlem as in other parts of the city." By the end of 1930, 50 percent of the African-American population in

W. E. B. Du Bois was among those hardest hit by the economic depression of 1929. In The Crisis, he urged African Americans to exploit racial segregation by becoming independent of white financial and political assistance.

Harlem was out of work.

Black churches and institutions such as the National Urban League did their best to ease the suffering. In several cities, the league established job-training programs and community centers for the needy. League workers found families housing, distributed clothes, fought evictions, provided loans, and set up programs for better playgrounds and public health.

The efforts of black churches were even more crucial. In Harlem, the United Holy Church of America unquestioningly offered food and clothing to needy families. Harlem's largest black church, the 8,000-member-strong Abyssinian Baptist Church, also contributed heavily to ease the distress.

The church was headed by the Reverend Adam Clayton Powell Sr., a charismatic and committed clergyman who grew up in the South, took over midtown New York's Abyssinian Baptist Church in 1908, and moved it to Harlem in 1922. When the depression hit, Powell demanded that black churches, including his own, do more for the needy. "The ax is laid at the root of the tree," he thundered, "and this unemployed mass of black men, led by a hungry God, will come to the Negro churches looking for fruit and finding none, will say cut it down and cast it into the fire."

Although the Depression did not immediately affect authors like Hughes and Hurston, who were still under the patronage of Charlotte Mason, it effectively ended the Harlem Renaissance. Harlem would go on, but its glory days were over. "The rosy enthusiasms and hopes of 1925 were . . . cruelly deceptive mirages," Alain Locke wrote in an August 1936 article for *Survey Graphic*. In a reversal of his claim in *The New Negro*, he went on, "There is no cure or saving magic in poetry and art for . . . precarious marginal employment, high mortality rates, civic neglect."

Indeed, poverty not only struck the ordinary Harlemite but ended the careers of many of the period's artists as well. Most black artists had always felt uncomfortable with the necessity of enlisting or accepting financial support from whites. When once-wealthy patrons who saw their funds reduced by the depression gave up their black artist and poet protégés, it became painfully clear how important such funding had been to black artistic success. Claude McKay would bitterly attribute the entire movement to the passing interests of white Americans: "The Harlem Renaissance . . . was really inspired and kept alive by the interest and presence of white bohemians," he maintained. "It faded out when they became tired of the new plaything."

Du Bois was among the movement's members who were severely affected by the depression. He lost his home and forfeited his life insurance. In 1930 he wrote to Cullen, to whom he owed money, "I am sorry that I have not kept my promise of remittances to you. . . . We have felt [the depression] especially in *The Crisis*, and I have not drawn my salary for several months in order to make things go."

The depression also intensified Du Bois's radicalism. He filled the pages of *The Crisis* with proposals to combat the dire economic situation through the "co-operation and socialization of wealth." The black population, he said, could not expect the aid of whites during a time of crisis. It was therefore essential that blacks pool their resources and support black enterprises—in effect, they should use racial segregation to their own advantage. Separate racial institutions did not have to mean racial discrimination.

Du Bois's call for "voluntary segregation" in the January 1934 issue of *The Crisis* greatly upset the members of the NAACP's executive board, who were opposed to the idea of segregation in any form. None was more annoyed than Walter White, who had replaced James Weldon Johnson in 1931 as the association's executive secretary. White had done extensive work for the NAACP by posing as a white man in the South (he was extremely fair-skinned), and although he may have been the epitome of the Talented Tenth, he did not agree with many of the editor's doctrines.

White attacked Du Bois's position on segregation in the March 1934 issue of *The Crisis*. Moreover, he reprimanded its editor for publishing an opinion that was not backed by the association. Du Bois countered by picking apart White's explanation of the NAACP's stand on segregation.

Augusta Savage at work on her monumental sculpture, The Harp, *which was commissioned by the New York World's Fair of 1939. Inspired by black spirituals and in particular by James Weldon Johnson's poem "Lift Every Voice and Sing," Savage's 16-foot sculpture depicts 12 stylized black singers as the strings of an enormous harp, whose sounding board is the hand and arm of God.*

But arguing was of little use. By that time, the circulation of *The Crisis* had decreased considerably, and the journal was losing money. On May 21, 1934, the NAACP's board of directors voted that "*The Crisis* is the organ of the Association and no salaried officer of the Association shall criticize the policy, work, or officers of the Association in the pages of *The Crisis*." Upon hearing the decision, Du Bois resigned. Although the NAACP praised Du Bois for creating "what never existed before, a Negro intelligentsia," Du Bois had been pressured to leave the journal in the hands of an organization whose leaders, he said, "have neither the ability nor the disposition to guide it in the right direction." He later wrote that resigning his position "was like giving up a child."

In the wake of the depression, many key figures of the Harlem Renaissance began leaving the area. *Opportunity* editor Charles S. Johnson had already accepted a position in 1928 as head of the social sciences department at Fisk University (he would later become the university's first black president). James Weldon Johnson joined him three years later as a professor of English at Fisk, and in 1937, Aaron Douglas became a professor of art there.

In a landmark presentation at the First American Artists Congress in 1936, Douglas wryly commented on the fleeting interests of white Americans in black art. The Harlem Renaissance, he said, was a time when "unsuspecting Negroes were found with a brush in their hands [and] were immediately hauled away and held up for interpretation." However, African-American art would continue, despite the passing fancies of white patrons. Those who painted before the Renaissance, he suggested, would continue to paint after its demise.

Langston Hughes returned from Cuba in 1931 to a country transformed by economic depression and a Harlem in financial ruin. Newspapers recorded tales of collapsed businesses and despairing citizens committing suicide, and bread lines snaked around city blocks. Charlotte Mason still sponsored Hughes, yet he could not dismiss the fact that without her financial support, he could easily become one of the many unemployed or homeless people he saw every day on the street. That winter, he published a caustic poem, "Advertisements for the Waldorf-Astoria," that parodied an advertisement for the new and socially exclusive New York hotel. Addressing Harlem, he wrote:

Say, you colored folks, hungry a long time
in 135th Street—
    they got swell music at the Waldorf Astoria. It
    sure is a mighty nice place to shake hips in, too.
    There's dancing after supper in a big warm room.
    It's cold as hell on Lenox Avenue. All you've had
    all day is a cup of coffee. Your pawnshop
    overcoat's a ragged banner on your hungry
    frame. . . .

Drop in at the Waldorf this afternoon
for tea. Stay for dinner. Give Park Avenue a lot
of darkie color—free for nothing! . . .
    Hallelujah! Undercover driveways!
    Ma soul's a witness for de Waldorf-Astoria!

            . . . .

(And a million niggers bend their backs on rubber
plantations,
    for rich behinds to ride on thick tires to the
    Theatre Guild tonight.)
        Ma soul's a witness!
(And here we stand, shivering in the cold, in
Harlem.)
    Glory be to God—
    De Waldorf-Astoria's open!

Not surprisingly, Godmother Mason did not appreciate the poem's message—nor Hughes's changing mood. By the late 1920s the hope and optimism felt by the black literati only a few years earlier had given way to boredom and weariness, and Hughes was among those who felt guilt and anger over his escape from the hardships of the depression. Moreover, he had begun keeping company with his friend and former typist, Louise Thompson, who with her circle of friends saw the Soviet Union's political system as a symbol of hope and a model for action.

As Hughes became more political, he began to disappoint Mason with his lack of productivity. Soon she would shut him out of her world entirely. Having won a prize from the Harmon Foundation, Hughes again traveled to Cuba and to Haiti. The trip did not alleviate his disappointment and feelings of rejection. "That spring for me (and I guess all of us) was the end of the Harlem Renaissance," he would later declare. "We were no longer in vogue, anyway, we Negroes. Sophisticated New Yorkers turned to [white playwright and composer] Noel Coward."

Zora Neale Hurston had moved to Florida in 1932, and the following year she was on the verge of being evicted for nonpayment of rent when a wire arrived—with a $200 advance payment—announcing that Lippincott had accepted her novel *Jonah's Gourd Vine*. "I never expect to have a greater thrill than that wire gave me," she recalled delightedly. The novel, loosely based on Hurston's own family life, was published in May 1934 and has been considered the last great novel of the Harlem Renaissance.

One member of the artistic community who did not leave Harlem was Augusta Savage. The Savage Studio of Arts and Crafts operated from her basement apartment on West 143rd Street, and with a $1500 grant from the Carnegie Foundation, Savage continued to create works of art.

Perhaps remembering her father's disapproval of her early efforts, Savage also dedicated herself to involving the children of Harlem in creative endeavors. When her librarian friend Anne Judge Bennis complained about delinquent children, Savage encouraged her to bring them to the studio. "They ought to know there are black artists," Savage said. She would become a mentor for a number of important African-American artists, including Norman Lewis, Elton C. Fax, and Ernest Crichlow. Artist Romare Bearden praised Savage, declaring that her "special stature among Harlem's young artists" came from her willingness to live "in their midst instead of disappearing 'downtown.'"

Perhaps no event signaled the end of the movement more than the death of A'Lelia Walker. To reduce her growing debts during the depression, the woman that Hughes had dubbed "the joy goddess of Harlem" had mortgaged her country home in 1930, to the dismay of Harlemites who had been privileged to attend her sumptuous gatherings. "White Buyers Strip Villa of Treasures," read the front page of the *Amsterdam News.* A year later, Walker, who suffered from high blood pressure, died suddenly at age 46.

Carl Van Vechten was allegedly too devastated to attend the funeral services for Walker. Even in death, the elegant matron of the black elite attracted attention: Langston Hughes noted that her body, dressed in a gold lace-and-tulle dress with a green velvet sash, was laid to rest in a silver casket. With Reverend Powell presiding, 15,000 New Yorkers came to pay their respects, and when the band played Noel Coward's "I'll See You Again," Hughes noted that "they swung it slightly, as she might have liked it." The Dark Tower was closed forever. "[It] was really the end of the gay times of the New Negro era in Harlem," said Hughes ruefully.

Two years later, in 1934, Wallace Thurman, one of the greatest successes of the Harlem Renaissance, died penniless in Welfare City Island hospital at age 32. The author of three novels, two screenplays, and a hit Broadway play had been defeated by alcoholism. The group of young writers who had shocked Harlem with *Fire!!* was growing smaller.

Although the Great Depression effectively ended the Harlem Renaissance, it could not destroy the era's artistic, political, literary, and musical legacy. Not only are many of the renaissance's works and artists still tremendously respected and influential today, but their example and their success opened doors for generations of future black artists. Countee Cullen, who returned to his high school alma mater to teach French, told tales of people like Langston Hughes and Arna Bontemps, and inspired at least one of his students—James Baldwin—to pursue a writing career. In 1910, black artists had little chance for recognition, but by 1930, publishing a novel by a talented black writer or producing a record by a talented black musician was simply seen as good business.

Dorothy West was 18 years old when her first short story won a prize in the *Opportunity* magazine contest of 1925. West moved from Boston to Harlem and befriended Thurman, Hughes, and other renowned members of the Harlem Renaissance. In 1935 she founded a literary magazine called *Challenge*, in which she published the work of colleagues and friends like McKay, Hurston, and Cullen. In 1943, she moved to Martha's Vineyard, a family vacation spot, and in the spirit of the Harlem Renaissance published *Living Is Easy*, one of the few novels published by an African-American woman during the 1940s.

Drawing on the themes of Fauset and Larsen, *Living Is Easy* relates the story of Cleo Jericho Judson, an ambitious and beautiful young southern woman, a sharecropper's daughter who "never had to be taught how to hold her head high . . . and how to keep her right hand from knowing what her left hand was doing." Cleo moves to Boston and trades on her light skin and classic features to break into the black elite community.

A lively black woman negotiating the conflicts of color and class with determination, Cleo defied the traditional stereotypes of black women as either controlling matriarchs or passive victims. "Back in 1948, a leading woman's magazine refused to publish chapters from my first book . . . because they feared losing subscribers," West recalled. "You see, no one knew what to make of my heroine because the word 'feminist' had hardly been invented yet. I didn't know she was a feminist until years later."

Not until 1995, when West was 87 years old, did she publish her second novel, *The Wedding*. Americans had mostly forgotten the young writer who had never achieved the fame of Langston Hughes or Zora Neale Hurston. However, West was hailed as the last living member of Harlem Renaissance.

"As a child, I decided I never wanted to be the last leaf on the tree, and now here I am, the last leaf," she mused. "I was a member of the Harlem Renaissance, you know, and the youngest person is the one who lives the longest."

FURTHER READING

Anderson, Jervis. *This Was Harlem: A Cultural Portrait*. New York: Farrar, Straus & Giroux, 1982.

Bearden, Romare, and Harry Henderson. *A History of American Artists*. New York: Pantheon, 1993.

Bloom, Harold, ed. *Black American Poets and Dramatists of the Harlem Renaissance*. New York: Chelsea House Publishers, 1995.

_____. *Black American Prose Writers of the Harlem Renaissance*. New York: Chelsea House Publishers, 1994.

Candaele, Kerry. *Bound for Glory 1910-1930: From the Great Migration to the Harlem Renaissance*. Philadelphia: Chelsea House Publishers, 1997.

Fauset, Jessie Redmon. *There Is Confusion*. Boston: Northeastern University Press, 1989.

Huggins, Nathan. *The Harlem Renaissance*. London: Oxford University Press, 1971.

_____. *Voices from the Harlem Renaissance*. New York: Oxford University Press, 1976.

Hughes, Langston. *Not Without Laughter*. New York: Scribner, 1969.

Hughes, Langston. *Selected Poems of Langston Hughes*. New York: Vintage, 1987.

Lewis, David Levering, ed. *The Portable Harlem Renaissance Reader*. New York: Penguin, 1994.

_____. *When Harlem Was in Vogue*. New York: Oxford University Press, 1989.

Locke, Alain, ed. *The New Negro*. New York: Atheneum, 1992.

McKay, Claude. *Home to Harlem*. Boston: Northeastern University Press, 1987.

Rampersand, Arnold. *The Life of Langston Hughes*. New York: Oxford University Press, 1986.

Rummel, Jack. *Langston Hughes*. New York: Chelsea House Publishers, 1988.

Stafford, Mark. *W. E. B. Du Bois*. New York: Chelsea House Publishers, 1989.

Studio Museum, The. *Harlem Renaissance: Art of Black America*. New York: Abrams, 1987.

Tolbert-Rouchaleau, Jane. *James Weldon Johnson*. New York: Chelsea House Publishers, 1988.

Walker, Alice, ed. *I Love Myself When I Am Laughing . . . and Then Again When I Am Looking Mean and Impressive: A Zora Neale Hurston Reader*. Old Westbury, NY: Feminist Press, 1979.

Watson, Steve. *The Harlem Renaissance: Hub of African-American Culture, 1920-1930*. New York: Pantheon, 1995.

West, Dorothy. *Living Is Easy*. New York: Quality Paperback Books, 1996.

INDEX

Abyssinian Baptist Church, 20, 112-13

"Advertisements for the Waldorf-Astoria" (Hughes), 117

Anderson, Regina, 62, 77

Anderson, Sherwood, 49, 51

Anti-Lynching Crusaders, 34

Armstrong, Louis "Satchmo," 18

Art and artists, 65-72, 77-81, 96, 103-7, 116

Aspects of Negro Life: An Idyll of the Deep South (Douglas), 72

Aspects of Negro Life: The Negro in an African Setting (Douglas), 72

Autobiography of an Ex-Colored Man, The (Johnson), 44

Baker, Josephine, 31

Baldwin, James, 120

Ballad of the Brown Girl, The (Cullen), 53

Bearden, Romare, 119

Bennett, Gwendolyn, 62, 77, 81

Bently, Gladys, 22

Bethune, Mary McLeod, 33

Big Sea, The (Hughes), 37, 55-56, 57

Black and White Club, 17, 83

Black Christ and Other Poems, The (Cullen), 54

Blake, Eubie, 16

"Blue Meridian" (Toomer), 52

Blues, 18-20, 21, 84, 87

Blues: An Anthology (Handy), 87

Bontemps, Arna, 12, 59, 63, 103, 120

Book of American Negro Poetry, The (Johnson), 44, 45

Braithwaite, William Stanley, 52

Bronzeville (Motley), 96

Brownies' Book, The, 42-43, 88

Calloway, Cab, 21

Cane (Toomer), 49-50, 52, 74

Caroling Dusk (Cullen), 53

Challenge, 120

Chinaberry Tree, The (Fauset), 75

Churches, 20, 28, 29, 54, 112-13

Church on Lenox Avenue (Johnson), 65

Civic Club, 74

Clubs, 14-15, 17-18, 19-21, 28, 63, 74, 83

Color (Cullen), 53

Color Struck (Hurston), 11, 63, 102

Comedy, American Style (Fauset), 75

Connie's Inn, 18, 20

Copper Sun (Cullen), 53

"Cordelia the Crude" (Thurman), 101

Cotton Club, 17, 21

Covarrubias, Miguel, 83

Crisis, The, 10, 32, 41, 42, 43, 44, 55, 57, 74, 75, 76, 114-16

Cullen, Countee, 10, 15-16, 43, 53-54, 55, 57-58, 63, 88, 94, 97, 100, 102, 114, 120

Cullen, Frederick, 15-16

Darker the Berry, The (Thurman), 101

Dark Princess (Du Bois), 35

Dark Tower, 15, 119

Darkwater (Du Bois), 74

Dean, Mrs. John. *See* Pig Foot Mary

Dill, Augustus, 42

Douglas, Aaron, 62, 72, 77, 100, 103-5, 116

"Drenched in Light" (Hurston), 63

Du Bois, W. E. B., 9, 32, 33, 34-35, 37, 39-43, 44-45, 46, 54, 55, 57, 74, 76, 80, 93-94, 96-97, 99, 102, 106, 114

Du Bois, Yolande, 54

Dunbar, Paul Laurence, 44

Durante, Jimmy, 21

East St. Louis, Illinois, race riot, 30

Edmund's Cellar, 19-20

Elegaic Poem, on the Death of that Celebrated Divine, and Eminent Servant of Jesus Christ, the Reverend and Learned George Whitefield, An (Wheatley), 61

Ellington, Edward Kennedy "Duke," 16, 17, 21

Europe, James Reese "Big

Jim," 31

Fauset, Jessie Redmon, 10, 42, 43-44, 45, 55, 57, 62, 63, 74, 76, 77, 81, 88, 93, 100

15th Regiment, 31

Fine Clothes to the Jew (Hughes), 37, 89

Fire!!, 73, 91, 100-103, 120

Fisher, Rudolph, 29, 84, 87

Fisk University, 39-40, 116

Fitzgerald, Ella, 31

Fitzgerald, F. Scott, 16

Ford, Ellis, 80

Frazier, E. Franklin, 10-11

Future Expectations (Wedding Day) (Van Der Zee), 106-7

Gamin (Savage), 80-81

Garvey, Marcus, 80

Gillespie, Dizzy, 31

God's Trombones (Johnson), 104

Great Depression, 109-20

Great Migration, 26-27, 29

Gurdjieff, Georgi Ivanovitch, 52-53

Handy, W. C., 21, 87

Harlem Home News, 28

Harlem Orchestra, 106

Harlem Property Owners Protective Association, 28

Harlem Renaissance, definition of, 12-13

Harlem Shadows (McKay), 38, 74

Harlem String Quartet, 16

Harlem Symphony, 16

"Harlem Wine" (Cullen),

54

Harper, Frances Ellen Watkins, 61-62

Harris, Lillian. *See* Pig Foot Mary

Hayden, Palmer, 68-69, 105

Henderson, Fletcher, 16, 17-18, 19

Home to Harlem (McKay), 95-96

Hopkins, Pauline E., 62

"House in Taos, A" (Hughes), 89

Houston, Texas, race riot, 30-31

"How It Feels to Be Colored Me" (Hurston), 23

Hughes, Langston, 10, 11, 12, 15, 19, 35, 37, 39, 43, 53, 55-59, 62, 64, 73, 76, 77, 87-92, 93, 94, 96, 99, 100, 102, 104, 113, 116-18, 119, 120, 121

Hurst, Fannie, 64

Hurston, Zora Neale, 11, 19, 23, 46, 54-55, 62, 63-64, 73-74, 81, 86, 90, 91, 99, 100, 102, 104, 113, 118, 120, 121

"If We Must Die" (McKay), 38

Infants of the Spring (Thurman), 86

Iola Leroy; or, Shadows Uplifted (Harper), 62

Janitor Who Paints, The (Hayden), 69

Jazz, 16-18, 22, 31, 84

Jim Crow laws, 21

Jitterbugs (III) (Johnson), 67

"John Redding Goes to Sea" (Hurston), 46

Johnson, Charles S., 9, 12, 15, 45, 62, 64, 74, 77, 84-85, 94, 103, 104, 116

Johnson, Hall, 16

Johnson, Helene, 103

Johnson, James P., 16

Johnson, James Weldon, 10, 15, 32, 38, 44-45, 84, 87, 92, 93, 99, 104, 114, 116

portrait of (Waring), 70

Johnson, William H., 65-67, 105

Jonah's Gourd Vine (Hurston), 118

Jungle Alley, 20-21, 22

Knopf, Alfred, 12

Krutch, Joseph Wood, 34

Ku Klux Klan, 33

Larsen, Nella, 62, 75-77, 81, 87, 94, 100

Lewis, David Levering, 18, 43, 94

Lindsay, Vachel, 10

Living Is Easy (West), 120-21

Locke, Alain, 35, 46-47, 55, 74, 77, 84, 89, 90, 94, 99, 102, 104, 113

Long Way from Home, A (McKay), 38

Lynchings, 33-34

McKay, Claude, 34, 37-38, 43, 44, 49, 50, 53, 74, 87, 95-96, 101, 113, 120

MacNeil, Hermon A., 79

INDEX

Marinoff, Fania, 83
Martin, Alfred W., 78-79
Mason, Charlotte Osgood, 47, 89, 95, 96, 104-5, 113, 116-17
Mencken, H. L., 10, 84
Mezzrow, Mezz, 19
Midsummer Night in Harlem (Hayden), 68
Mills, Florence, 16
Morton, Jelly Roll, 18
Motley, Archibald, 96, 105-6
Mules and Men (Hurston), 74
Music, 16-21, 22, 31, 34, 84, 87
Musicals, 16
Nance, Ethel Ray, 62, 63, 64, 77
National Association for the Advancement of Colored People (NAACP), 10, 34, 44, 54, 83, 86
National Urban League, 9, 112
"Negro Artist and the Racial Mountain, The" (Hughes), 89
"Negro Speaks of Rivers, The" (Hughes), 56-57
Nelson, Alice Dunbar, 33
Nest Club, The, 20
"New Negro," 15, 75, 84, 85-86, 107
New Negro, The, 102, 104, 113
New York Age, 38, 44
New York Public Library,

Harlem branch of, 16, 57, 80
Niggerati, 86, 99-100
Nigger Heaven (Van Vechten), 92-96
Nugent, Richard Bruce, 64, 100, 101-2
Oliver, Joe "King," 18
O'Neill, Eugene, 10, 12, 16
Opportunity: A Journal of Negro Life, 9-12, 15, 58, 63, 77, 84-85, 87, 116, 120
Ory, Edward "Kid," 18
Outlet, The, 100
Parker, Charlie, 31
Passing (Larsen), 76
Payton, Philip A., Jr., 27, 28
Philadelphia Negro, The (Du Bois), 41
Photography, 106-7
Pig Foot Mary, 28-29
Plum Bun (Fauset), 75
Portrait of Paul Bustill Robeson as Othello (Reyneau), 71
Powell, Adam Clayton, Sr., 113, 119
Prohibition, 21-22
Quicksand (Larsen), 76
Race relations, 15, 20-22, 30-35, 37, 40-43, 75, 76, 78-80, 84, 85, 93, 99
Race riots, 30-31, 32, 37
Rainbow Orchestra, 18
Rampersand, Arnold, 10, 87
Reiss, Winold, 103-4
Rent parties, 22-23

Reyneau, Betsy Graves, 71
Rhone, Arthur "Happy," 17, 83
Riis, Jacob, 27
Robeson, Paul Bustill, 12, 16, 77, 86-87
portrait of (Reyneau), 71
Salem Methodist Episcopal Church, 54
Savage, Augusta, 62, 77-81, 105, 118-19
Savage Studio of Arts and Crafts, 81, 118
Savoy Ballroom, 18
Scott, Emmett J., 79
"Shroud of Color" (Cullen), 10
Shuffle Along, 16
Sissle, Noble, 16
Smith, Bessie, 19
"Smoke, Lilies and Jade" (Nugent), 101-2
Souls of Black Folk, The (Du Bois), 37, 40
Spingarn, Arthur, 75
"Spunk" (Hurston), 11, 63
Still, William Grant, 16
"Stompin' at the Savoy," 18
Street Life, Harlem (Johnson), 66
Survey Graphic, 104, 113
Sweat (Hurston), 102
Talbert, Mary B., 33, 34
Talented Tenth theory, 40-41, 43, 44-45, 46, 114
Tanner, Henry Ossawa, 79, 103
Theater, 16, 34
There Is Confusion (Fauset),

74, 75
Thurman, Wallace, 23, 86, 94, 99, 100-101, 119-20
"To a Brown Boy" (Cullen), 55
Toomer, Jean, 43, 49-53, 62, 74
Trotter, William Monroe, 42
Tucker, Earl "Snakehips," 22
Tucker, Louella, 62
Tuskegee Normal and Industrial Institute for Blacks, 41
Underwood, Edna Worthley, 12
Van Der Zee, James, 106
Van Doren, Carl, 74

Van Vechten, Carl, 11-12, 83-84, 86-88, 92-96, 101, 119
Walker, A'Lelia, 14-15, 93, 119
Walker, C. J., Madame, 14, 28
Waller, Fats, 16, 20
Walrond, Eric, 62, 63
Waring, Laura Wheeler, 70
Washington, Booker T., 41, 44
Waters, Ethel, 19-20, 62, 87
"Weary Blues, The" (Hughes), 10, 15, 58-59
Weary Blues, The (Hughes), 87
Wedding, The (West), 121
Wells-Barnett, Ida, 33, 41-

42
West, Dorothy, 120-21
Wheatley, Phillis, 44, 61
White, Gladys, 83
White, Walter, 15, 33, 46, 92, 114
Wilson, Woodrow, 30
Women, in Harlem Renaissance, 10, 11, 19-20, 23, 33, 41-42, 43-44, 45, 46, 54-55, 57, 61-64, 73-81, 86, 87, 88, 90, 91, 93, 99, 100, 104, 113, 118, 119, 120, 121
Woollcott, Alexander, 10
World War I, 26, 30, 31, 32, 33, 75, 85
YMCA, Harlem branch of, 16

VERONICA CHAMBERS lives in Brooklyn, New York. She is the author of *Mama's Girl*, a memoir, and co-author with John Singleton of *Poetic Justice: Filmmaking South Central Style*. A former editor at the *New York Times Magazine*, Chambers has also written for many national magazines, including *Premiere*, *Glamour*, *Essence*, and *Seventeen*. She has held a fellowship at the Freedom Forum Media Studies Center.

PICTURE CREDITS

page

2-3: Corbis-Bettmann

8-9: Corbis-Bettmann

11: Photographer Collection, Moorland-Spingarn Research Center, Howard University

13: The Walker Collection of A'Lelia Bundles

14: Corbis-Bettmann

17: New York Public Library

18: Corbis-Bettmann

20: New York Public Library

24-25: The Schomburg Center For Research in Black Culture, NYPL, Astor, Lenox and Tilden Foundations

26: Library of Congress, neg. # LC-USF33-20598

30: Underwood & Underwood/Corbis-Bettmann

32: UPI/Corbis-Bettmann

35: Prints & Photographs Collection, Moorland-Spingarn Research Center, Howard University

36: Archives of the University of Massachusetts at Amherst

39: Library of Congress, neg.# LC-J694C

42: The Schomburg Center For Research in Black Culture, NYPL

44: The Schomburg Center For Research in Black Culture, NYPL

47: The Schomburg Center For Research in Black Culture, NYPL

48: UPI/Corbis-Bettmann

50: Library of Congress, neg. #USZ62-26015

52: The Schomburg Center For Research in Black Culture, NYPL

55: The Schomburg Center For Research in Black Culture, NYPL

56: Corbis-Bettmann

60: The Schomburg Center For Research in Black Culture, NYPL

63: The Schomburg Center For Research in Black Culture, NYPL

65-67: National Museum of American Art, Washington DC/Art Resource, NY

68: Museum of African American Art, Los Angeles, CA

69: National Museum of American Art, Washington DC/Art Resource, NY

70-71: National Portrait Gallery, Smithsonian Institution/Art Resource, NY

72: (top & bottom) Art & Artifacts Division, The Schomburg Center For Research in Black Culture, NYPL, Astor, Lenox and Tilden Foundations

74: Beinecke Rare Book & Manuscript Library, Yale University

76: The Schomburg Center For Research in Black Culture, NYPL

77: The Schomburg Center For Research in Black Culture, NYPL

79: Beinecke Rare Book & Manuscript Library, Yale University

80: National Museum of American Art, Washington DC/Art Resource, NY

82-83: New York Public Library

85: (l & r) Beinecke Rare Book & Manuscript Library, Yale University

86: Photographer Collection, Moorland-Spingarn Research Center, Howard University

89: The Schomburg Center For Research in Black Culture, NYPL, Astor, Lenox and Tilden Foundations

91: The Schomburg Center For Research in Black Culture, NYPL

92: Beinecke Rare Book & Manuscript Library, Yale University

95: Bernice Abbott/Commerce Graphics Ltd. Inc.

98: Beinecke Rare Book & Manuscript Library, Yale University

101: (l) Beinecke Rare Book & Manuscript Library, Yale University, (r) Photographer Collection, Moorland-Spingarn Research Center, Howard University

102: Corbis-Bettmann

106: photo by James VanDerZee, © 1997 by Donna VanDerZee

108: Archives of Labor & Urban Affairs, Wayne State University

110-111: photo by James VanDerZee, © 1997 by Donna VanDerZee

112: The Schomburg Center For Research in Black Culture, NYPL, Astor, Lenox and Tilden Foundations

115: The Schomburg Center For Research in Black Culture, NYPL